—— ALL ABOUT ——
GARDEN WILDLIFE
OF AUSTRALIA

GARRY SANKOWSKY

First published in 2015 by Reed New Holland Publishers Pty Ltd
London • Sydney • Auckland

The Chandlery, 50 Westminster Bridge Road, London SE1 7QY, UK
1/66 Gibbes Street, Chatswood, NSW 2067, Australia
5/39 Woodside Avenue, Northcote, Auckland 0627, New Zealand

www.newhollandpublishers.com

A record of this book is held at the British Library and the National Library of Australia.

ISBN 978 1 92151 751 8

Managing Director: Fiona Schultz
Publisher and Project Editor: Simon Papps
Designer: Thomas Casey
Production Director: Olga Dementiev
Printer: Toppan Leefung Printing Ltd

10 9 8 7 6 5 4 3 2

Keep up with New Holland Publishers on Facebook
www.facebook.com/NewHollandPublishers

——— ALL ABOUT ———

GARDEN WILDLIFE OF AUSTRALIA

GARRY SANKOWSKY

ACKNOWLEDGEMENTS

Thank you to my wife Nada for doing the initial editing for spelling, typos and grammar.

PHOTOGRAPHIC ACKNOWLEDGEMENTS

All images taken by the author, except for the following. The generosity of these photographers in providing images for this book is greatly appreciated.

Lorraine Harris: p.13 Wompoo Fruit-Dove, p.15 Topknot Pigeon, p.18 Victoria's Riflebirds displaying, p.31 Red Wattlebird, p.34 Rainbow Lorikeet (left), p.37 Galahs, Red-tailed Black Cockatoos (above left), p.39 Red-rumped Parrot, p.40 Budgerigars, p.43 Common Bronzewing, p.45 Zebra Finch (below), p.54 Lumholtz's Tree-Kangaroo, Musky Rat-Kangaroo, p.64 Echidna, p.66 Olive Python, p.71 Boyd's Forest Dragon, p.79 Spotted Marsh Frog; **Steve Hitchcock**: p.15 Pied Imperial Pigeon (below left), p.17 Green Catbird, p.23 Golden Whistler, p.26 Grey Fantail, p.27 Blue-faced Honeyeater, p.39 Red-winged Parrot, p.41 Emerald Dove, p.42 Wonga Pigeon, p.43 Bar-shouldered Dove, p.78 Great Barred Frog, p.79 Salmon-striped Frog; **Jenny Thynne**: p.5 Garden Jumping Spider, p.21 Superb Fairy-wrens, p.57 Common Ringtail Possum, p.71 Eastern Water Dragon (below), p.91 Leafcutter Bee, p.93 Yellow Hairy Flower Wasp, p.94 Ichneumon Wasp (left), p.102 Robber Fly with butterfly prey, p.104 Green Stink Bug, p.107 Common Bluetail Damselfly, p.114 Common Lynx Spider, p.115 Garden Jumping Spider, Green Jumping Spider; **Tony Morris**: p.21 White-browed Scrubwren, p.52 Red-necked Pademelon, p.55 Long-nosed Bandicoot, p.59 Koalas, p.62 Grey-headed Flying-fox (below), p.65 Red-bellied Black Snake (above left), p.67 Diamond Python; **Patrick Kavanagh**: p.19 Mistletoebird, p.21 Brown Thornbill, p.22 Striated Pardalote, Scarlet Robin, Red-capped Robin, p.23 Rufous Whistler, Golden Whistler, p.24 Crested Shrike-tit, Weebill, p.3 Rainbow Bee-eater, p.25 Rainbow Bee-eater, Shining Bronze-cuckoo, Pallid Cuckoo, p.26 Dusky Woodswallow, Masked Woodswallow, White-browed Woodswallow, Welcome Swallow, p.32 Brown-headed Honeyeater, p.35 Musk Lorikeet, p.38 Crimson Rosella, Eastern Rosella, p.39 Superb Parrot, p.45 Zebra Finch (above); **Don Franklin**: p.27 Noisy Friarbird, p.28 Eastern Spinebill, p.30 Noisy Miner, p.35 Scaly-breasted Lorikeet, p.36 Sulphur-crested Cocktaoo, p.38 Pale-headed Rosella, p.42 Crested Pigeon, p.44 Crested Pigeon, p.51 Eastern Grey Kangaroo, Rufous Bettong, p.52 Red-necked Wallaby, Swamp Wallaby, p.55 Northern Brown Bandicoot, p.57 Yellow-bellied and Sugar Gliders, Sugar Glider, p.63 Little Red Flying-fox, p.68 Skink (above left), p71 Frill-necked Lizard, p.72 Lace Monitor; **Rigel Jensen**: p.73 Burton's Legless Lizard, p.76 Red Tree Frog (below right), p.77 Stony Creek Frog, p.78 Green-striped Frog; **John Skewes**: p.38 Western Rosella, p.130 Rainbow Lorikeet bathing; **Andrew Thornhill**: p.75 White-lipped Tree Frog (right); **David Rentz**: p.110 Chirping Field Cricket; **Lloyd Nielsen**: p.124 and p.125 diagrams of nest boxes, p.126 table of dimensions of nest boxes. **Used under Creative Commons licence: Sydney Oats**: p.27 New Holland Honeyeater; **Lip Kee Yap**: p.32 New Holland Honeyeater (left); **Derek Midgley**: p.32 New Holland Honeyeater (right); **Julla Gross**: p.32 Western Spinebill; **Ron Knight**: p.33 Singing Honeyeater (left); **Wayne Butterworth**: p.33 Singing Honeyeater; **Vijay Chennupati**: p.69 Blue-tongue Lizard; **Peter Mackay**: p.88 Emperor Gum Moth.

CONTENTS

AN INTRODUCTION TO GARDEN WILDLIFE

THE WILDLIFE YOU SEE in your garden will depend on many things, including where you live, how large your garden is, how many native plants it contains and many more factors that will be discussed later in the book.

Even the smallest suburban garden will contain some wildlife such as lizards and insects, and the proximity to natural bush or rainforest will determine the diversity of the species you are likely to see. If you are lucky enough to live on a rural residential block of one hectare or more you have the opportunity to attract a wide range of wildlife and this also will be discussed in detail later in the book.

Birds and butterflies are the two groups that can be observed easily as they are active during the day. Many Australian wildlife species are only active at night (they are nocturnal) so you will need to go spotlighting to see what is really around. As well as being nocturnal most of our animals are secretive and can easily be missed. Ground-dwellers such as wallabies are easily frightened, so dogs running around will most likely scare them off.

Even a small suburban garden can have a range of wildlife if it is reasonably close to a park. While many parks contain a lot of exotic (introduced) plants they will usually have enough native species to harbour some interesting creatures.

Many species are seasonal in their habits. Most insects breed only in the summer and many birds migrate to different parts of Australia, or beyond, for the winter. In the cooler areas most reptiles slow down or go into hibernation for the coldest periods. This is not always a bad thing as snakes tend to disappear or become very scarce during the winter.

A lot of enjoyment can be attained by simply observing the wildlife that visits your garden. Later sections of this book give details of how to enhance your garden so many more species will be attracted. With careful planning it is also possible to exclude most pest species of birds such as sparrows and mynas.

The larger your garden area the more diverse it can be made. An island of vegetation can attract much more wildlife than a garden up against the natural bush. If your garden has the correct environment and size many species will live there permanently, whereas if your garden is part of the natural bush it is just a small part of a larger system and species will tend to come and go.

WHAT WILDLIFE AM I LIKELY TO SEE IN THE GARDEN?

THERE ARE MANY FACTORS that govern what can be seen in any particular garden or backyard. For instance, if you live beside natural bush or rainforest you can expect many species to visit your garden from these areas. What time you look for wildlife is also critical as most of our mammals are nocturnal, and while you may find some of them sleeping during the day you have a much better chance of observing them at night-time.

The following chapters will look in some detail at the different types of garden wildlife that may be encountered. While it is well beyond the scope of this book to identify every single species you may see, you should be able to pin-point a group into which they fit, such as whether a lizard could be a skink, dragon, gecko, goanna, or even a legless variety.

A reasonably good pair of binoculars is essential but you do not have to spend a huge amount of money. The best for watching wildlife have a magnification of 7–10x and an objective lens of 30–50mm, so suitable specifications could be 7x30, 8x40, 10x50, and so on. Reasonably good models by a range of companies can be found for about AUD$100–200, but you can pay a lot more for some of the really top-quality brands.

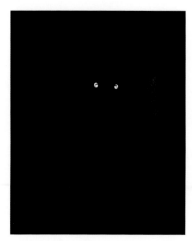

On the left are a pair of Brushtail Possum eyes viewed from a distance – on the right is what you see when you get closer.

For night observations a good modern LED headlight is the best. Some of the cheap models perform fairly well but the top of the range is the German-made Ledlenser brand. The one I use has a range of 200 metres, runs on just four AA batteries and costs about AUD$130. The main features you need are:

Variable beam focus – spread out for walking, map-reading and when you are close to an animal so as not to blind it.

Rechargeable batteries – this is absolutely essential as it cuts the cost of running the light down to almost nothing. Good brand-name NIMH batteries can be charged at least 500 times and at about AUD$25 for four of them this works out to about 5 cents per charge. Brand-name alkaline batteries will cost you at least AUD$4 per set if you buy them in bulk, or more if you buy them one set at a time.

There are a couple of advantages in using a headlight. The obvious one is that your hands are free, but the main advantage is that your eyes are always aligned with the beam. By having the light close to your eyes you can see the light reflected back from the eyes of any wildlife and you will soon learn to recognise the different groups by the reflected colours. Probably the most surprising ones are spiders. The eyes of even tiny ones sparkle like emeralds, and you will be amazed at how many there are all around you.

GARDEN BIRDS

BIRDS WILL PROBABLY BE the first form of wildlife you will notice in your garden, so it seems sensible to start by covering this group first.

Birds have the same advantage as many insects, in that they have wings and can fly (except for a few notable exceptions such as Emus and Cassowaries). This means that they can move quickly and easily when in search of new areas in which to feed or live. The changing seasons and varying weather patterns mean that quite a lot of bird species move around. With the seasons some species move north or south and a reasonable number go way beyond Australia when our winter arrives. Most 'complete' birds of Australia books (such as *The Slater Guide to the Birds of Australia*) will give you detailed information on these migrations, such as when they leave and when they are likely to return. Droughts in inland Australia will often force inland birds towards the coast. One year in our garden we saw Diamond Doves. Usually this is only a temporary situation but sometimes birds may stay if the food supply is abundant. Galahs have done this in a number of areas and like any seed-eating parrot can become a pest in commercial grain crops.

Cyclones often cause the relocation of many bird species. One year we had a flock of Frigatebirds pass over, about one day ahead of the arrival of a cyclone. This is extremely unusual as we are on the Atherton Tablelands in north Queensland. After Cyclone Larry in 2006 we had a Wompoo Fruit-dove arrive and take charge of a fruiting Umbrella Tree, chasing away all other birds that came to feast on it. At the same time White-cheeked and Bridled Honeyeaters appeared for the first time. The interesting thing is that these three species came back the next year at the same time. The Wompoos visit spasmodically and the White-cheeked Honeyeaters stopped coming after a few years but the Bridled Honeyeaters continue to arrive each year around April and stay to breed. This shows the amazing memory that birds have for location of food supplies and time of the year.

Waterbirds are the least likely birds that you will see in the garden, unless you live on the shores of a dam or lake. For those people that live in such a situation it is a good idea to have lawn going down to the water. This will encourage ducks and other species to wander up onto the lawn and rest. Many people living on the shores of Lake Tinaroo on the Atherton Tablelands enjoy these birds in this way.

You will need to consult a 'complete' birds of Australia book such as the

Slater guide to identify every single species in the following groups that are in your area. The first thing you should look at when identifying any wildlife is the distribution map so you are not trying to match a bird with one that does not occur in your location.

The basic groups are:
- Fruit-eaters
- Insect-eaters
- Nectar-feeders
- Seed-eaters

WHAT ARE THE FRUIT-EATING BIRDS?

A wide range of birds eat fruit as well as other foods; this chapter deals with the species that feed mostly on fruit. The largest fruit-eating bird is of course the Southern Cassowary, but as very few people are lucky enough to have this bird visiting their garden it has not been included in this book.

 Fruit-eaters do an excellent job of spreading the seed of the plant species they feed on. Birds that utilise fruit for most of their diet (Figbirds, for example) usually do not have a gizzard as chickens do, so the seeds in the fruit they eat are not ground to pulp and germinate readily when they pass through their system.

The largest fruit-eating bird which can fly is the **Channel-billed Cuckoo**. It ranges from the Kimberley around the top of Australia and down the eastern half of the country to Victoria, rarely making it as far south as Tasmania. Each autumn they migrate north, reaching the Celebes to the west and at least New Ireland to the east. In September or October they return to Australia, their southern route taking them along paths where fig trees grow, providing an abundance of fruit. They usually travel along streams or through patches of dry rainforest where fig trees are common.

 Like most cuckoos they do not build their own nest but deposit their eggs in nests of large birds like Magpies, Crows or Currawongs.

 They have an incredibly loud, harsh call that can be heard from a great distance. As well as fruit they also will eat insects and eggs or the young of other birds.

 In north Queensland they are often called 'storm birds' because they arrive at the start of the storm season, but this name should be reserved for the Eastern Koel as its call is heard almost non-stop throughout the storm season.

Female Eastern Koel.

Male Eastern Koel.

The **Eastern Koel** also migrates north in autumn and returns to Australia in September or October. The pair that occupy our garden arrive like clockwork on about the 22nd October and stake out specific fruiting plants, claiming them for themselves, although the male and female usually select a different plant. They often call day and night, upsetting some people, but I like the call, it is the sound of summer and heralds the start of the stormy season. The male's call can get quite frantic at the approach of a low-pressure system.

While birds like the large Honeyeaters chase the male, the female slips eggs into their nest. Friarbirds seem to be alert to the dangers posed by the female Koel and often chase her, causing her to shriek at the top of her voice.

The distinctive call of the beautiful **Wompoo Fruit-Dove** can be heard throughout the tropical and sub-tropical rainforests of eastern Australia down to about the Victoria border. They feed in the trees and utilise any fruit that they can swallow whole. Surprisingly the fruits of the Blue Quandong (*Elaeocarpus grandis*) fall into this category. If you live in or near these rainforests you will have heard this bird calling.

The **Superb Fruit-Dove** is the most striking of the fruit-eating pigeons. The bright purple crown seems a most unusual colour for an Australian bird. As you would expect, this bird eats small fruit and in the tropical rainforests where it occurs these are in abundance. In our garden they often feed on the small juicy fruits of *Psychotria* bushes, thus presenting themselves right down to eye-level.

The juveniles and females lack the beautiful colours of the adult male. The juveniles are mostly green and the females have a small blue patch on the head, with a green back and a creamy-white underside.

When they are not breeding they rarely call and you do not know they are around unless you see them.

More often than not the **Brown Cuckoo-Dove** is seen eating the fruit of the introduced Tobacco plant. They are found all along the east coast of Australia where there is moist to wet rainforest, down as far as Victoria.

Usually they feed up in the trees and they have the ability to flop around amongst the fruit and foliage on the outside of the plant, but if necessary they will descend to the ground to pick up fallen fruit and gravel to assist their gizzard function. The male calls from prospective nesting sites to win the approval of the female.

The **Topknot Pigeon** is found in rainforest along the east coast of Australia down as far as Victoria. Large flocks of non-breeding birds move around in search of plentiful supplies of fruit. Big numbers of them arrive in south Queensland when the *Archontophoenix* palms are in fruit. They regurgitate the seeds and often as a flock passes over it rains palm seeds.

Like the Brown Cuckoo-Dove they have the ability to land on the outside of trees, where most of the fruit is found.

The **Pied Imperial-Pigeon** (also known as the Torresian Imperial-Pigeon or Torres Strait Pigeon) is a common sight during the summer months in lowland areas of tropical Australia, even in the centre of Cairns, feeding and nesting in trees planted in parks and gardens. Their deep and powerful *coo-hoo* call can be heard from quite some distance away as they raid the fruits of numerous rainforest plants. Breeding colonies on offshore islands can be very large, containing 20,000 or more birds.

Male Figbird.   *Female Figbird.*

In northern and eastern Australia, in an area stretching from the Kimberley to Victoria, **Figbirds** are one of the best-known of the fruit-eating birds. The northern form of the male, pictured above, is very brightly coloured. They often move around in small flocks and breeding pairs do not seem to mind their territory being invaded by these flocks. They do not usually make their nests in fruiting trees but sometimes build very close to such a food-source.

The **Olive-backed Oriole** can easily be mistaken for a Figbird but the red eye gives it away. They are found throughout northern and eastern Australia south to Adelaide. Their diet is mainly fruit but they sometimes take insects. Their call often sounds like the ringing of a distant phone.

16

Spotted Catbird. *Green Catbird.*

Catbirds are found in rainforest habitats – the Green Catbird occurs from about Gympie to Victoria and the Spotted Catbird from Cape York to Townsville. Catbirds are not afraid of people and will readily raid fruit such as Pawpaws in a garden.

The **Satin Bowerbird** is strictly a rainforest species in the tropical part of its range, but further south it can be found in a much wider variety of habitats and it is not uncommon in suburban gardens in Sydney. It occurs as far south as Melbourne.

The male builds a substantial bower, usually decorating it with blue objects. In suburbia, blue clothes pegs are a favourite treasure.

This species eats a wide range of fruits and will readily take a handout from a tray in the garden.

Male Satin Bowerbird. *Female Satin Bowerbird.*

17

The **Victoria's Riflebird** is found in the tropical rainforests of north Queensland, usually occurring above altitudes of about 500m. The adult males (top left) put on a spectacular display but juvenile males (top right) are often seen practising. As is usually the case with brightly coloured male birds the rather dull coloured female (above) raises the young on her own.

They eat a wide range of fruit and are particularly fond of Pawpaws. Anyone growing this fruit and living near the upland rainforest of north Queensland has a hard time beating the birds to the fruit.

The Paradise Riflebird, which is found in the rainforests of south-east Queensland and northern New South Wales, is very similar.

Male Mistletoebird.   *Female Mistletoebird.*

The beautiful little **Mistletoebird** is found in all states except Tasmania, from the coast to the dry inland. As well as Mistletoe fruit it eats many small fruits such as figs and *Psychotria* berries.

The **Silvereye** is a very small bird but is not restricted to eating fruit it can swallow. When faced with a large food item they simply pick the fruit apart as the one on the left is doing with a large fig. They are found in eastern, southern and south-western Australia.

The **Macleay's Honeyeater** often eats more fruit than nectar. Anyone who lives where this bird is found and puts out fruit for birds will find this species one of the first to line up for a feed.

WHAT ARE THE INSECT-EATING BIRDS?

While most Honeyeaters and even some Finches eat insects at times, there are quite a number of other bird species that rely heavily on insects in their diet. In this chapter a selection from this group is displayed. Insect-eaters can usually be identified by their behaviour as they search for their food.

This is a very diverse group and covers a wide range of species. There is also a big variation in the way these birds find their insects, some of them are:

- searching through the foliage and unrolling curled-up leaves
- lifting up loose bark
- foraging in the leaf litter
- darting out and snapping insects from mid-air.

Usually, the older and more established your garden is the more insect-eating birds there will be.

Fairy-wrens, Scrubwrens, Thornbills, Weebills and Pardalotes are some of the very small birds that visit gardens. Most of these small birds become accustomed to having people near them and can often be observed at quite close quarters.

Superb Fairy-wrens. There is at least one blue or red Fairy-wren in all parts of Australia. They prefer grassy or dense low shrub areas. Often common in gardens.

Large-billed Scrubwren. Scrubwrens are found along the east coast in rainforest or nearby wet sclerophyll forest.

White-browed Scrubwren is widespread from north Queensland to south-west Western Australia.

Brown Thornbill occurs from central Queensland to Adelaide and Tasmania.

Male Spotted Pardalote.   Female Spotted Pardalote.

These beautiful little birds are found in eastern and southern Australia, including in Tasmania.

Spotted Pardalote on a home visit.   Striated Pardalote occurs Australia-wide.

The **Spotted Pardalotes** in our garden are completely unafraid of humans and will continue nest-building and feeding young when we are only a couple of metres away. They are also very curious. The male (above left) was fluttering at the windows and sliding door to our lounge so I opened the door to see what he would do. He flew into the room almost immediately, then hovered, like a helicopter, in the centre while slowly rotating, getting a good look around. Next he flew and sat on the back of a chair about one metre from where I was sitting, had a look around and flew out.

Male Scarlet Robin.   Female Scarlet Robin.   Red-capped Robin.

Scarlet Robin is often common in gardens and is found from south-east Queensland to Adelaide, Tasmania and south-west Western Australia. This striking little bird is found over the southern two-thirds of Australia but is absent from Tasmania. It will often feed very close to people, showing no fear. **Red-capped Robin** is widespread in the southern and central Australia.

Eastern Yellow Robin is found from about Cooktown to Adelaide but not in Tasmania. It is often the first bird to start the dawn chorus.

Grey-headed Robin is confined to the wet tropics area of Queensland, usually in rainforest.

Female Rufous Whistler. *Male Rufous Whistler.*

The **Rufous Whistler** is found throughout mainland Australia.

Male Golden Whistler. *Female Golden Whistler.*

The **Golden Whistler** is found from about Cooktown to Adelaide, in Tasmania and also in the south-west corner of Western Australia, ranging west of the Great Dividing Range but not in the dry inland.

Fairy Gerygone is found from Cape York to about Rockhampton in rainforest and nearby Eucalyptus woodland.

The tiny **Weebill** occurs throughout mainland Australia in a wide variety of habitats.

The **Crested Shrike-tit** has several races and is found from the top end of Western Australia, Northern Territory and north Queensland south to Adelaide and also in the south-west corner of Western Australia.

Black-faced Monarch is found in eastern Australia, from Cape York to Melbourne, in rainforest, mangroves and eucalypt forests. These birds migrate north to Papua New Guinea and surrounds for the winter. A few juveniles sometimes remain in the north of Australia during the winter.

The **Grey Shrike-thrush** is found throughout Australia and five races are recognised.

The beautiful **Rainbow Bee-eater** is found throughout mainland Australia. Southern breeding populations are summer migrants from the north.

The **Shining Bronze-cuckoo** migrates during summer from the islands north of Australia to the eastern half and the west coastal regions where it breeds. They eat a wide range of insects, foraging both in the foliage and on the ground.

Male Pallid Cuckoo.

Pallid Cuckoo occurs throughout Australia and is particularly noticeable during spring and summer when it is calling. It hunts insects in the foliage and on the ground and like most of the larger insect-eating Cuckoos it can eat hairy and toxic caterpillars that other birds leave alone.

Grey Fantail is found throughout Australia – southern populations migrate north for the winter.

Willie Wagtail is one of our best-known birds and is found in all states.

Dusky Woodswallow is found in eastern and southern Australia, usually occurring in groups. They rest and sleep clustered together.

Masked Woodswallow is found over most of mainland Australia. They also operate in groups.

White-browed Woodswallow can occur in very large flocks and is found in all states.

Welcome Swallow occurs Australia-wide – it is often seen sitting in rows on wires.

WHAT ARE THE NECTAR- AND POLLEN-FEEDERS?

These include Honeyeaters, Lorikeets and species such as the Spangled Drongo, Silvereye and others that take nectar from time to time. As well as nectar some Honeyeaters also eat insects, fruit and seeds with a fleshy coating. These requirements will be covered in more detail in the section dealing with attracting more wildlife to your garden.

Honeyeaters

A bird in this group can usually be identified by its long decurved bill, which is designed especially for probing into flowers.

The largest members of this group are the Friarbirds but they are certainly not the most beautiful. They tend to be fairly aggressive and often chase other species away from their favourite flowering tree. Various species are found over northern and eastern Australia.

Many Honeyeaters have a similar range, which includes most of northern and eastern Australia. The south-west corner of Western Australia has a number of its own species but these are still easily recognised as Honeyeaters by the characteristic decurved and pointed bill.

The Noisy Friarbird lives up to its name with consistent noisy chatter.

The Blue-faced Honeyeater is also a large bird that is found over most of northern and eastern Australia.

New Holland Honeyeater on flowers of the Red-capped gum in Western Australia.

Eastern Spinebill feeds only on nectar and is nomadic in pursuit of flowering shrubs, especially Melaleucas.

Lewin's Honeyeater – as well as nectar this species eats fruit, insects and seeds with oily or fleshy coatings.

Yellow-faced Honeyeater feeds on nectar and insects.

Macleay's Honeyeater is strictly tropical. It feeds on nectar, insects and fruit. Watch your pawpaws when they are ripe!

Brown Honeyeater is found over most of Australia except Victoria and Tasmania. It has one of the most beautiful songs of all the group and can be heard along streams and rivers where bottlebrushes grow, as well as in gardens which feature Grevilleas and Melaleucas.

Bridled Honeyeater (right) is confined to north-eastern Queensland and feeds on insects, nectar and fruit. This species is noisy and aggressive but in our garden plays second fiddle to the Lewin's Honeyeaters.

One of the most spectacular of all honeyeaters is the **Scarlet Honeyeater**. The images above show how the beautiful red colour develops as the bird ages. Large non-breeding flocks follow the flowering trees, especially Melaleucas, and at times as many as 50 or more can be feeding in one tree. This makes a truly spectacular sight with the bright red and black of the mature male birds standing out against the white flowers.

Noisy Miner is found over most of eastern Australia and if it occurs in your area it will be very obvious. This is one of the few native birds than can become a pest in suburban areas. For this reason it should never be fed. It is an extremely aggressive bird and when the numbers build up in a region it chases out many other species, attacking them as a 'gang' and even killing smaller birds.

They feed mainly on insects and other small invertebrates but take nectar and fruit readily when available. They become very cheeky and will enter houses in search of food.

Apart from being a pest because they chase out other birds they can also cause considerable damage to stone fruits and grapes when they invade farming areas.

Like most species when in their natural habitat they fit into the environment without causing undue problems.

White-throated Honeyeater is a bird of the open Eucalypt forest but groups of them visit our artificial rainforest garden each day to drink and bathe. It is probably the whole family that comes as there are usually about four of five of them at once. They feed on insects as well as nectar, usually high up in the trees. The bird-bath is the best place to observe them as they arrive in a group and really enjoy a good bath.

Red Wattlebird is fond of insects, large spiders, nectar and fruit. It occurs in south-eastern and south-western Australia, inhabiting forest and woodland areas. Non-breeding flocks move around in search of nectar. During this time they may attack stone fruit orchards but they do not usually occur in high enough numbers to cause serious damage. They can become very aggressive and should not be encouraged to visit bird feeders.

Yellow Honeyeater is found in northern and central Queensland, extending well inland at the northern end of its range. It has a very loud call and if it is in your area you are usually aware of it. They feed on insects and nectar.

Brown-headed Honeyeater is confined to southern Australia from about Rockhampton southwards but is not found in the south-west corner of Western Australia. They feed on insects and nectar and form non-breeding flocks in search of food.

The very handsome **New Holland Honeyeater** is another southern species which ranges from south-east Queensland to the south-west of Western Australia, but is missing from the Great Australian Bight and the drier inland areas. It feeds on both insects and nectar; nomadic groups move around in search of flowering trees.

Female Western Spinebill.

Western Spinebill is confined to the south-west corner of the continent. It is common within its range, utilising the vast array of flowering shrubs and trees in this region. The male has a white stripe above and below the eye, as well as fringing the buff-coloured area on his chest, followed by a black band.

Singing Honeyeater is found west of the Great Dividing Range all the way to the Western Australian coast, but not in Tasmania. This bird does not always live up to its name but at times in the dawn chorus it is very vocal. The Brown Honeyeater would have been a more suitable candidate for this name. As well as nectar it eats fruit and many types of insects, both the adults and larval stages. The Singing Honeyeater is one of the few species with a distribution that covers most of Australia.

Lorikeets

Lorikeets occur in northern, eastern and southern Australia but not in the very dry inland. They are generally quite noisy and rarely feed in silence. When flocks of them are feeding they screech and zoom around at break-neck speed. They are all brightly coloured, although their base colour is green.

Eucalyptus flowers are probably their favourite but they will feed on almost any suitable flowering shrub or tree. Melaleucas are used extensively throughout their range but in the tropical rainforest *Melicope elleryana*, *Melicope bonwickii* and Umbrella Trees attract large flocks.

Even though they are primarily nectar- and pollen-feeders they will feed on seed, especially when this is placed out for birds in peoples' gardens. When nectar is in short supply they will resort to eating lerps. A lerp is the crystallised honeydew produced by larvae of psyllid insects as a protective cover. These insects are often very common on Eucalyptus trees and can sustain local populations of lorikeets when no plants are in flower.

The **Rainbow Lorikeet** is probably the best-known of this group and is commonly seen in large flocks feeding on Melaleuca and Eucalyptus flowers from Cape York to Adelaide. They range well inland from the coast, several hundred kilometres, but do not make it to the centre of Australia. They often hop along rather than walk, which makes them look quite comical at times.

The very similar Red-collared Lorikeet occurs in the top end of Northern Territory and Western Australia. It has a red or orange band on the back of the neck, as opposed to the yellow band of the Rainbow Lorikeet. It was formerly considered a subspecies of the Rainbow Lorikeet but today most authorities 'split' it as a separate species in its own right.

The beautiful little **Musk Lorikeet** inhabits the south-eastern part of Australia, including Tasmania. Pairs often join together to form flocks while feeding. Like most of their relatives they continue to chatter while feeding.

The **Scaly-breasted Lorikeet** is probably more often heard than it is seen. It is found along the east coast of Australia, but not in Tasmania. Feeding flocks fly rapidly through the trees screeching loudly but with a higher-pitched call than the Rainbow Lorikeet. As well as nectar and pollen they take fruit, especially grapes and stone-fruit, also seed, especially the unripe milky grain of sorghum.

WHAT ARE THE SEED-EATING BIRDS?

Seed-eating birds cover a very wide range in size, from large Black Cockatoos to small finches. There will be birds that feed on seed in all parts of Australia and this chapter covers a good selection so you should be able to recognise the ones in your area that fall into this group.

The Cockatoos are the largest birds in this group and they all have several things in common – they feed primarily on seeds and make their nests in hollow limbs.

Sulphur-crested Cockatoo is probably the best-known cockatoo and is found over a wide area of Australia from about Broome in north-west Western Australia all the way round to Adelaide, including northern Tasmania.

This cockatoo is common in the rainforest as well as in the dry inland but does not get to the very dry centre of the country. As well as eating seed from dry fruits they rip open many rainforest fruit species to extract the seed. They can become a pest in commercial fruit-growing areas, sometimes attacking Citrus or Mango crops. Similarly they can impact heavily on commercial grain crops, even peanuts when they are pulled.

The magnificent **Red-tailed Black Cockatoo** has a number of races and is found in many parts of Australia, including the dry inland. They are nomadic and large flocks move around in search of seeds. It is quite remarkable that with their huge beak they are able to extract the tiny seed from Eucalyptus fruit. They sometimes feed on the large grub of a gall wasp that infests Bloodwood trees, just one bite with their massive beak can extract the grub from the rock-hard gall.

Sometimes this beautiful bird is a pest on grain crops. They have a particular liking for sorghum and when the crop was mature at Lakeland Downs clouds of them would appear. Hand-raised birds are often sold as pets (see top right image).

Being found Australia-wide the **Galah** is very well known by most Australians. Large flocks roam in search of seed and they will often stay as long as the food supply lasts. They usually eat seed from the ground, waiting until it has fallen rather than extracting it from fruit on the tree as many other parrots do.

Rosella Parrots

There are about eight species of Rosellas with at least one species for each state, including Tasmania. As well as eating dry seed they extract seed from small fruit, especially Dianellas, and often pull off a flower and eat the ovaries, containing the developing seed.

Pale-headed Rosella occurs from Cape York to northern New South Wales.

Crimson Rosella is found from Cooktown to Adelaide in rainforest and wet sclerophyll.

Eastern Rosella ranges from south-east Queensland to Adelaide.

Western Rosella inhabits south-west Western Australia.

Adult male.   *Immature.*

Australian King-parrot occurs from Cooktown to Adelaide. It is confined to rainforest in the tropics but its range extends well inland further south.

Red-winged Parrot is found in northern and eastern Australia south to about the Victoria border.

Australian Ringneck. Various races cover most of Australia except for northern and eastern regions. Not found in Tasmania.

Superb Parrot is found in Eucalypt forest in inland New South Wales and Victoria.

Red-rumped Parrot occurs in New South Wales, Victoria and to about Adelaide in South Australia.

The **Budgerigar** is probably Australia's most well-known parrot, being kept as a cagebird all over the world. They occupy most of Australia south of the Gulf of Carpentaria and west of the Great Dividing Range, except for Tasmania. They are often seen in huge flocks and move on when a seed supply runs out.

Pigeons and Doves

Most pigeons and doves have a separate crop and gizzard, as do domestic chickens. The crop stores and softens the seed, which is then ground to a pulp in the gizzard. This means no viable seed passes through these birds. Almost all of them search the ground for fallen seed and spend most of the time walking, rather than flying. They also pick up stones which help to grind up the seed in the gizzard.

The beautiful **Emerald Dove** feeds mostly on seed but will also take fruit. I have seen them sitting on a log picking Dianella berries from the plant but mostly they search the ground for fallen seed and fruit. They are common over northern and eastern Australia down to Victoria and regularly visit suburban gardens.

Wonga Pigeon is Australia's largest seed-eating pigeon. It is found from central Queensland to Victoria and occurs in both rainforest and eucalypt forest. A very loud flapping of wings is heard when this bird takes off from its usually ground-feeding position. Their early morning call can be heard from a great distance in the still air.

Crested Pigeon is well-known over most of Australia, being absent only from some of the 'top end'. When it flies it creates a loud whistling and flapping noise that is very distinctive. If your chicken coop has no cover this pigeon will often drop in to have a free lunch with the chickens.

Preparing for the night.

Peaceful Dove occurs over the eastern half of Australia, excluding Tasmania, as well in the north-western part of Western Australia. When night-time comes pairs of them often huddle together on a branch. They are easily disturbed when sleeping so tread lightly if spotlighting.

42

Bar-shouldered Dove occupies northern and eastern Australia, extending partway into Victoria but not to Tasmania. The nest, top right, is more substantial than that of most pigeons and the eggs in it are quite secure. Many pigeons make nests so flimsy that if the sitting bird is startled the eggs fall to the ground.

Common Bronzewing, which occurs Australia-wide, is another pigeon that makes a very loud flapping noise when flying, especially on take-off. They often gather in numbers on fields, where farmers grow cover crops of legumes, to pick up the leftovers when the crop is ploughed in. This one is getting a free handout in a garden.

43

When you see a pigeon bowing and cooing like the **Crested Pigeon** on the left it is the alpha male displaying his authority. They will usually do this a few times then chase one or more other males (or even other species) away when they are too close. Sometimes they will spend so much time chasing other males away that one wonders when they actually get time to feed.

Sometimes the Peaceful Dove gets aggressive with smaller birds like Finches and actually attacks them, not exactly living up to their name.

The **Red-browed Finch** is found in eastern Australia and inhabits a variety of habitats including the edge of rainforest. They feed mostly on seed but also take small insects.

If you live within their range they are easily attracted to the garden by placing suitable seed (such as Budgie seed) out for them.

Finches become very friendly and will often take seed from your hand.

Finches are common over most of Australia but only one species, the Beautiful Firetail, is found in Tasmania.

The **Zebra Finch** is found in all mainland states but prefers the more open and drier habitats. On rare occasions they visit our garden, probably when the seed supply further west is in short supply.

WHERE DO BIRDS NEST?

MANY SMALL TO MEDIUM-SIZED BIRDS nest low down in shrubbery and bushy trees, often from one to three metres from the ground, but some nest high up in trees, including on bare branches, while others nest on the ground. Some nests are heavily camouflaged while others are easy to spot. Nests will often be placed so they cannot be seen from above – this helps protect against raids by hawks.

Usually bird nests are difficult to find, but if you see a bird carrying some nesting material you may be able to observe where the nest is being built. It is best not to go too close to the nest and you should never touch it, the human smell left behind can lead predators like possums and snakes to the nest.

This Little Shrike-thrush is carrying some nesting material. It was very wary and did not go near the nest while I was watching.

Often the first indication you have that birds have nested is spotting a fledgling like this Eastern Yellow Robin.

The **Fairy Gerygone** on the left is gathering nesting material the easy way – stealing it from the nest of a Large-billed Scrubwren. It is not uncommon for birds to do this. I have observed Red-browed Finches dismantling the nest of some Double-barred Finches and making their own nest out of the material.

If you have shrubs and trees near your house you may be surprised at just how close to the house some birds will build their nests.

This Brown Cuckoo-Dove made its nest in a hanging basket in our pergola, just outside a bedroom window.

Strange as it may seem a pair of Spotted Pardalotes used the same basket to make their nest. The image on the right shows the entrance for the nest from above. They used this nest twice and did not seem to be put off by the automatic watering system that came on every day.

A pair of **Grey Shrike-thrushes** nested in this piece of machinery in the garage of a friend. They used this same site for two years running.

It seems that quite a few birds are keen to take advantage of man-made shelters.

47

This Fairy Gerygone nest was also in our pergola. Another year they built a nest just outside a lounge-room window.

A rather untidy nest belonging to a pair of Large-billed Scrubwrens. This is the nest from which the Fairy Gerygone was stealing.

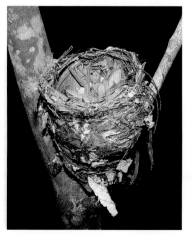

This rather neat little nest is that of the Eastern Yellow Robin. The outside is well camouflaged with bits of bark and lichen.

The eggs of the Eastern Yellow Robin can vary from this pale blue to quite a bright dark blue colour.

When sitting on the nest most birds keep a low profile but usually have a view out with one eye.

Figbirds usually nest fairly high up in trees, most frequently at heights of 5–10m. Mostly their structures are well hidden but I have seen one nest completely out in the open that came to grief in a storm.

Lewin's Honeyeaters build a very strong nest, usually between 1–3m off the ground. They go to incredible lengths to line the inside with very soft material. One pair I observed gathered kapok from a nearby tree for several days and stuffed it into the nest. This must have been the best-lined nest in history.

Many honeyeaters build quite close to the ground, usually in a well-sheltered position which is invisible from above. Some species build much higher – the White-throated up to 25m and the Yellow-tinted up to 30m.

This Bar-shouldered Dove is keeping a wary eye out from the nest.

GARDEN MAMMALS

ALMOST ALL OF OUR MAMMALS are nocturnal. While wallabies and kangaroos can be seen during the day they are much more active during the night. The further your property is from natural vegetation the fewer mammals you will see. They have numerous barriers to cross such as fences, busy roads and open space, as well as the potential for attack from dogs and cats. Rural residential developments will offer the best opportunities for mammals to access gardens; anyone in this situation should design their garden to maximise its attractiveness to this group.

Agile Wallabies. Wallabies and kangaroos need open space and grass. On rural residential properties in north Queensland this sight is common.

Agile Wallaby up close.

Kangaroos require even more space and have disappeared from many of the near-suburban areas where they once ranged. Even so, they are still a very common animal.

Rufous Bettongs on the other hand require very little space and get used to being near people. In our area of the Atherton Tableland they are very common.

Eastern Grey Kangaroo.

Rufous Bettong.

Red-necked Wallaby is found from central Queensland to south Australia and is also present in Tasmania.

Swamp or **Black Wallaby** has a wide distribution, from Cape York to Victoria.

Red-necked Pademelon is most common on the edge of rainforest where good supplies of grass are available. It ranges from central Queensland to central New South Wales. At times this species can become very common where introduced grasses have provided unlimited food.

Red-legged Pademelon female with joey.

The alpha male Red-legged Pademelon showing scars from territorial fights.

Red-legged Pademelon has a wide distribution, being found from Cape York to central New South Wales. They feed mostly on seedlings of rainforest plants but take grass when available. Because of their adaptation to eating non-grass species they can be a serious pest in the garden, eating every fern, orchid or shrub they can reach. Most gardeners who live near rainforest where this species occurs have fences all around their most precious plants.

Lumholtz's Tree-Kangaroo.

Tree-Kangaroos are confined to the rainforests of north Queensland between about Cardwell and Cooktown. On the Atherton Tablelands the Lumholtz's Tree-Kangaroo often crosses open paddocks to feed in gardens with a good selection of rainforest plants. On the ground they are rather awkward and vulnerable to dog attacks. Bennett's Tree-Kangaroo occurs from Daintree to Cooktown.

The rather secretive **Musky Rat-Kangaroo** will only be seen in your garden if it is adjacent to the north Queensland tropical rainforest. Unlike most of its relatives it is generally active during the day, in the early morning and afternoon. They feed on fruits and insects.

Northern Brown or **Common Bandicoot** is often considered a pest in gardens as it digs holes all over lawns and garden beds in search of grubs. They have a habit of digging in freshly disturbed soil where a tree has just been planted, uprooting it and causing its death if not discovered early next morning. They are found across the top end of Australia and down the east coast to central New South Wales.

Long-nosed Bandicoot is common in gardens throughout eastern Australia. The colour ranges from grey to brown and it does not grow as large as the Northern Brown Bandicoot.

Possums and **Gliders** are found in most areas of Australia, with the highest concentration being along the east coast. They usually eat leaves and flowers but some rainforest species are more specialised.

Common Brushtail Possum.

This Common Brushtail Possum is sharing some milk with the cat.

The best-known member of the family is the **Common Brushtail Possum**. It is found over most of the eastern half of the continent, as well as in the dry centre, Tasmania and south-west Western Australia.

It is omnivorous (it eats anything) with its diet ranging from leaves, flowers and fruit, to insects, birds' eggs and nestlings.

They generally roost in tree hollows but if they can get into the ceiling of a house this serves the same purpose. Because of this, and the fact that they eat any fruit you may try to grow, they are often considered a pest.

Sugar Glider (right), Yellow-bellied Glider (left).   *Sugar Glider.*

Sugar and **Yellow-bellied Gliders** often cut through the bark of certain Gum Trees to lick up the sap. They return to the same cuts night after night to make sure the wound is kept open and the sap flowing. The Yellow-bellied Glider is found in north Queensland then from central Queensland to Victoria while the Sugar Glider is much more widespread, ranging from the Kimberley region to south Australia and also in Tasmania.

Common Ringtail Possum.

The **Common Ringtail Possum** varies in colour from rusty (as in this image) to grey. It is found from Cape York to south Australia and also in Tasmania and south-west Western Australia.

They feed mainly on leaves and are particularly fond of the red and pink new growth of Gum and Lilly Pilly trees. They also eat fruit and flowers. Unlike most other possums they build a nest of leaves and grass.

Squirrel Glider.

The **Squirrel Glider** is usually found away from the coast, occurring in Eucalypt forest from about Cooktown to South Australia. They are similar to the Sugar Glider but larger and darker in colour.

Feather-tailed Glider.

The tiny little **Feather-tailed Glider,** no larger than a mouse, is found from Cape York to Adelaide and well inland. It occurs in the Eucalypt forest and will come to Callistemon and Grevillea flowers in a garden. This species is so tiny that it mostly goes unnoticed under the cover of darkness.

The iconic **Koala** is known to most Australians and is found in the eastern states south of about Cooktown. In the tropics they are not very common but have been seen as far inland as the Gilbert River. Being slow and awkward on the ground makes them vulnerable when crossing roads. Diminishing habitat near cities has made them quite scarce in many areas.

Koala.

It was a hard night!

Spectacled Flying-foxes in daytime roost.   *Spectacled Flying-fox.*

Flying-foxes or **Fruit Bats** have been given some bad press in recent years because of the Bat Lyssavirus. While there have so far been only three confirmed infections from this virus it is wise not to handle these animals if you should find one injured, in case it bites you.

Flying-foxes roost in very large colonies and fly great distances each night in search of food. They are major pollinators of flowers in both Eucalypt forests and rainforests. Their reputation for spreading seed is highly overrated as they usually take great care not to swallow seeds. When eating fruit they are basically juice extractors. They chew the flesh of the fruit for quite some time then spit out the fibre and any seeds. They are so efficient at juice extraction that the discarded fibre looks like cotton wool. When raiding a fruit tree they will often grab a fruit and fly to a nearby tree, away from the rest of the gang, and eat it there. The seed will then be dropped under that tree so the distance it is moved is quite small. Seed that they disperse by swallowing is only very small seed from fruit such as Figs.

Clearing of rainforest has greatly reduced the areas where they can roost and they often become unpopular when they choose an area close to or in a city. They can do a great deal of damage in orchards to fruit such as Mangoes and Lychees.

The **Spectacled Flying-fox** is confined to the eastern tropical coast of Queensland. They feed on blossoms and fruit, foraging long distances from their roosting site.

Apart from their usual diet they eat quite a lot of *Melaleuca leucadendra* bark and the leaves of *Albizia lebbeck*. *Albizia* leaves are very nutritious but the need for bark remains a mystery.

When sleeping they often hang by one foot, holding their other one across their stomach.

Miranda (Foxy Lady), the Grey-headed Flying-fox.

When we had the Butterfly Farm at Mt Tamborine, in the Gold Coast hinterland, we adopted Miranda after she had fallen off her mother as a baby. We had just received a case of Bowen mangoes from the Gulf Country so this was a big hit with her.

At this time Flying-foxes were a declared pest and thousands of them were shot by fruit-growers and any hooligan with a gun that felt like killing something.

We had Miranda for 11 years and kept her most of the time in the butterfly cage where she was a big hit with tourists. She was a great pet, purring like a kitten when stroked. She was quite choosy and ate only the best quality fruit.

The **Grey-headed Flying-fox** is found from central Queensland to Victoria and often several hundred kilometres inland. Like the Little Red Flying-fox they prefer blossoms but are not shy at taking fruit as well as insects.

Like other Flying-foxes they become quite unpopular when they set up a roosting camp in a city, having the reputation of being very dirty and smelly. In themselves they are very clean and spend a lot of time cleaning and grooming.

Contrary to popular belief they do not urinate or defecate on themselves, they reach up with their wings and swing their head up to take care of these chores. Thousands of any animal in the one area will be quite smelly.

Little Red Flying-fox.

The **Little Red Flying-fox** is very wide ranging, from central coastal Western Australia to Victoria, and up to 300km inland. They often roost in large colonies along streams where there is fairly dense vegetation. Their main diet is nectar and pollen but they also eat fruit if flowers are in short supply.

The **Tube-nosed Bat** is found in eastern Queensland, mainly occurring in rainforest, but they visit gardens quite regularly and usually roost in the garden until the fruit supply has finished. The tube-nose is very handy when eating fruit. As they chomp away the juice runs between their nostrils instead of up them. The short rounded jaw seems to make them dribble while feeding so they evolved tubed nostrils to solve the problem.

Tube-nosed Bat.

63

Short-beaked Echidna.

There is only one species of **Echidna** in Australia so it is not really necessary to use the full name. They occur Australia-wide and while they may not often be seen you can certainly see where they have been. They have enormous power in their claws and legs, being able to move rocks larger than themselves as they search for ants and termites. They eat many ants but not the ones that pack a sting.

When disturbed they dig in with their claws and roll up into a tight ball, creating an impenetrable barrier of spines. If they want to go through a fence they will either rip a hole through it or dig under it.

Defence pose.

GARDEN REPTILES

MOST PEOPLE DO NOT MIND LIZARDS in the garden but do not want snakes. One of the huge problems with snakes is making a correct identification. The colour varies enormously in many species and so colour patterns are not a reliable guide. Unless you are very familiar with snake species it is best to assume they are all dangerous and stay clear of them. Most Pythons are recognisable but not all have the familiar carpet pattern.

Red-bellied Black Snake is venomous but rarely deadly. It is widespread in the eastern states and reasonably easy to recognise.

The **Whip Snake** is mostly active during the day and not at all afraid of people. The very large eyes and slender body make it fairly easy to identify. The one on the left is drinking water from a drain on a hot day.

The **Bandy Bandy** is widespread though rarely seen. It operates at night and feeds mainly on blind burrowing snakes. This is a venomous species but is usually docile and presents no problem to humans if left alone. The markings make it easy to recognise.

Green Tree Snake.

The **Green Tree Snake** can be green, green with iridescent blue patches, yellow or almost black. The close-up image on the left shows the iridescent blue sheen on this dark form. They are active mostly at night although can often be seen during the day. They are not venomous and pose no threat.

Pythons are the largest of our snakes and while their bite is not poisonous they can be dangerous when very large as they crush their prey by coiling around it.

Olive Pythons are quite large, often reaching a length of four metres, and are fairly aggressive so they should be approached with caution. They are found across northern Australia in Eucalypt and Acacia woodlands, particularly along streams. This snake is a strong swimmer and often hunts in the water; the diet consists of wallabies, birds, other reptiles and frogs. It is an egg-laying snake and lays between 10–40 eggs at a time.

Olive Python.

Amethystine Python.

Amethystine Python occurs in northern Queensland and is found mostly in rainforest. It can grow to at least six metres in length. It is Australia's largest snake and can swallow prey as large as a medium-sized wallaby. The diet consists mostly of mammals, usually possums and tree-kangaroos. They have great patience and will wait outside a hollow for several days until a possum makes a desperate dash to escape; the snake usually gets its meal. This species is a danger to pets and can easily take cats and small dogs.

The **Carpet Python** is probably the best-known member of this group and is common in gardens. It can grow to at least three metres. Their colour patterns

vary considerably, sometimes being black and white. Small mammals and birds are their usual fare.

The **Diamond Python** is found in coastal New South Wales, and at the northern end of its range it occurs alongside the Carpet Python. It grows to about two metres and feeds on mammals and birds, including Flying-foxes.

Carpet Python.

Diamond Python.

Skinks are a very large group of lizards with nearly 400 species named in Australia, with more being identified and described all the time. Most of them are a similar shape and they can be easily recognised as a group.

Blue-tongue.

Among the largest members the skink group are the **Blue-tongues**. There are a number of different species that occur in various areas of Australia, so the one in your garden may not look exactly like the image above. They eat a wide range of food, including mushrooms, and are not shy about helping themselves to some leftover cat dries. Blue-tongues are widespread and there is a species for most regions of the country.

They are slow-moving so usually feed on prey that cannot escape easily. They have large teeth and strong jaws that can crush snail-shells and beetles.

If threatened they turn towards the threat, open their mouth and stick out their tongue. If the threat persists they flatten their body and hiss. Like most skinks they can throw their tail so they should never he picked up this way.

The **Shingleback** is confined to the southern half of the country. It occurs west of the Great Dividing Range in the dry inland. This slow-moving lizard is well known to many gardeners. The image below was taken in a garden near Perth.

Like the Blue-tongue they are rather slow so cannot chase very active prey. They eat leaves and mushrooms as well as insects and snails.

Shinglebacks usually live in open country where there is good ground-cover in which to hide. They usually rest under logs or other objects during the night and mainly hunt for food in the warmer parts of the day.

Shingleback.

Geckos are most frequently seen running across the ceiling or hunting moths on windows of homes. They have adhesive pads on their toes which enable them to get a grip on almost any surface. Unfortunately the Asian House Gecko has invaded the habitat of many of our northern species. It has a very loud call, unlike that of the Common House Gecko.

Ring-tailed Gecko.

Common House Gecko.

The **Ring-tailed Gecko** is confined to the north-eastern Tropics of Queensland and has distinctive colours, unlike the gecko species usually seen in houses.

The **Common House Gecko** (of which there are quite a few species) is usually welcomed into a house at first, but as their numbers build up and they start to make a mess all over the place their welcome fades.

The introduced Asian House Gecko has spines on the tail so is easily separated from native species that inhabit houses.

The positive side to geckos in the house is that they eat insects, thus aiding pest control.

Dragons are a group of small to medium-sized lizards. They have rough skin and most have spikes reminiscent of Dinosaurs. They inhabit all types of habitat from dense rainforest to the dry inland.

Frill-necked Lizard.

Eastern Water Dragon.

Boyd's Forest Dragon is found in the rainforests of northern Queensland and looks very much like a miniature version of its distant relatives, the Dinosaurs. Their colour varies but always matches the surrounding hues of its habitat.

Australia has about 70 species of Dragons and some of these can be seen even in the larger cities. They are very swift on their feet and often stand up on their hind-legs when they are really in a hurry.

Unlike Skinks, Dragons do not shed their tail when attacked, in fact, for small dragons, this is the best way to pick them up. Mostly well-camouflaged, they often do not run when approached slowly, hoping they will not be seen.

Boyd's Forest Dragon.

Goannas are found in all mainland states and are the largest of our lizards. They can move very fast and have a wide range of prey, including small mammals, lizards, snakes, birds and birds' eggs. They are well known by anyone keeping domestic chickens for their liking for chicken eggs. As well as live prey they are also fond of carrion and can be found feasting on dead animals.

Like most lizards they lay eggs, but they cannot re-grow limbs or tails like skinks.

LEGLESS LIZARDS

It is very difficult to tell this group of lizards from snakes. They have no forelegs but their greatly reduced and redundant hind-legs can be seen if observed closely. Because they look so much like snakes it is best to keep clear of anything resembling a snake unless you are very certain of the identity. There are about 40 species of legless lizards in Australia.

Burton's Legless Lizard.

Burton's Legless Lizard is found in all mainland states, being less common in the south-east corner of Australia. It has the unusual ability of being able to retract its eyes, which affords good protection when attacking its prey. It sometimes wriggles the tip of its tail to distract prey before striking.

It feeds mostly by day but can also be active during the night, usually ambushing its prey while hiding in leaf litter.

Most legless lizards eat insects but the Burton's Legless Lizard is a predator of other lizards.

GARDEN FROGS

IF YOU LIVE IN A DRY CLIMATE it does not necessarily mean there are no frogs in your garden. If there is a supply of water during the wet season some species will be able to breed. Some frogs do not even need a pond or creek, just pools of water in tree hollows.

Identifying frogs is at times quite difficult as many of them have a few different colour forms, and they can change their colour depending on the surroundings. For instance I have seen the Green Tree Frog turn bright yellow when it has been resting on a yellow raincoat, and an almost white Striped Marsh Frog when it was hibernating on a white plastic bag in a shed.

Two different colour variations of the common Green Tree Frog.

Dainty Tree Frog.   *Dainty Tree Frog.*

The **Dainty Tree Frog** comes in a variety of colours. It is a small frog that hibernates on the leaves of trees in the garden and their rather high-pitched call can be heard when the first rains start. They do not come down to mate and lay eggs until there has been very heavy rain and water is lying everywhere. The male on the bottom right of the previous page is performing the mating call, and many dozens of them in one area at the same time can create quite a din.

A common frog in the Queensland tropics is the White-lipped Tree Frog. These are two of the colour variations that can be found.

Some frogs actually hibernate under the ground by burrowing and living on the water stored in their body. They exude a slimy substance from their skin that forms a protective coating and helps prevent water loss. Before burrowing they take in large amounts of water which makes them big and round. The grey adult below has just come out of the ground after very heavy rain. Burrowing frogs can live in the dry inland and only emerge when rains are heavy enough for them to breed.

The extreme colour variation between adult and juvenile of this species shows just how hard it is to identify frogs. The book *Tadpoles and Frogs of Australia* by Marion Anstis will be of tremendous help in this regard.

Wide-mouthed or Eastern Snapping Frog.

Juvenile.

Red or Desert Tree Frog.

The **Red Tree Frog**, also sometimes called the Little Red Tree Frog, is very widespread and is found from Cape York to a line drawn from about Canberra to Geraldton in Western Australia. Their call is a distinct 'bleating' sound and they are certainly heard more often than seen. The one pictured at the top and left came out of hiding one night after heavy rain. Like geckos they sometimes come to windows to eat moths attracted to light.

They are quite small, measuring only from about 3–4cm, the females usually being larger than the males.

Female Stony Creek Frog.

Male Stony Creek Frog.

The range of the **Stony Creek Frog** is limited to the north-east Wet Tropics region of Queensland, from about Cooktown to Tully, including the Atherton Tablelands. The colour of the males varies a lot; some being completely yellow and others bright yellow and brown.

If you live in this region and have a permanent creek running through your property, look for them sitting on rocks at night.

77

Green-striped or Striped Burrowing Frog.

Green-striped Frog is a species that burrows into the ground to hibernate, coming to the surface after heavy rains. It is found throughout Queensland, extending into the gulf area of Northern Territory and the northern half of New South Wales.

Great Barred Frog's range is restricted to within 50km of the coast from about Mackay to central New South Wales. It is well camouflaged and forages at night amongst the leaf litter in the vegetation along streams.

Salmon-striped Frog is usually found away from the coast from about Bowen to southern New South Wales. It is a burrowing frog, remaining underground until heavy rains encourage it to emerge and start breeding. This species is often associated with dams on farms.

Spotted Marsh Frog is found in the eastern half of Australia, including Tasmania. This frog can breed at any time of the year and is quick to take advantage of any substantial rain event. It needs only a temporary pond or flooded drain to breed and makes the most of these situations.

GARDEN INSESCTS

INSECTS ARE THE MOST PROLIFIC life form on the earth. Butterflies are well known and beetles are fairly well known but most species in many of the other groups remain un-named. Some of the more interesting groups you may find are Bees, Flies, Bugs and Mantids. To give some idea of the enormous numbers involved there are about 7,500 species of flies named in 100 families and some scientists estimate that this represents only approximately 25 per cent of the actural numbers. There are about 30,000 species of beetles in Australia and only 20,000 of these are named.

BUTTERFLIES

Butterflies are the most likely insects you will see in the garden simply because they are often colourful and fly by day, even though there are only about 400 species in Australia. Moths are much more prolific; about 20,000 species in Australia with only 10,000 named. Because almost all of them fly by night they are seldom seen.

Because butterflies fly during the day they are easily observed. Most butterflies occur in the tropics so the number of species to be seen will diminish towards the south.

Butterflies and moths have a 'four-stage life cycle: egg, caterpillar, chrysalis and adult.

The following are some of the more common and widespread butterflies that can be seen in Australian gardens.

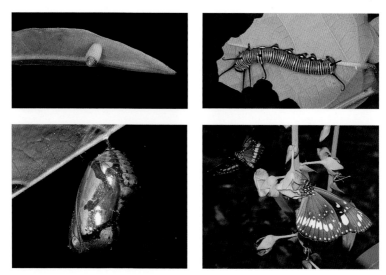

Life cycle of Common Crow butterfly.

Chequered Swallowtail.

The **Chequered Swallowtail** butterfly is found in all Australian states except Tasmania. The host plants are various species of Cullen, a small annual or perennial pea flowering herb or shrub, usually with blue or mauve flowers. These plants and the butterfly are very common in inland Australia and at times large migrations can be seen following good rains in the inland. The pupal stage can last for several years to survive long dry periods.

Male.   *Female.*

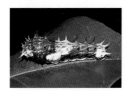

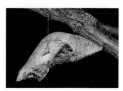

Orchard Swallowtail is found throughout eastern Australia. The larvae feed on many native plants in the Citrus (Rutaceae) family and because they frequently use cultivated Citrus their range has greatly increased in the last 200 years. They have been found in Darwin and Alice Springs so will probably eventually populate all mainland states.

Even though the larvae of this butterfly eat cultivated Citrus trees they do not become a pest because natural predators and parasites keep them under control.

The pupae can be either green or brown, depending on background colours when the larva is pupating.

Dingy Swallowtail is not a rainforest butterfly: it is found in the open forest over the eastern half of Australia. The natural host plants are native Citrus, a couple of which grow in the very dry inland. Because it has adapted to cultivated Citrus it is now very common over most of its range. The female lays her eggs only on the very new shoots of the plant when it is growing in the full sun. The males and females have the same markings.

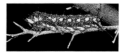

Dingy Swallowtail.

Male.

Female.

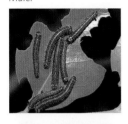

The **Caper White** butterfly occurs Australia-wide, being scarce in Tasmania and the south-west of Western Australia. The larvae feed on native caper trees as well as on the cultivated commercial Caper plant. They will eat all species of *Capparis* but as they are essentially a butterfly of the open forest they are less common in rainforest. Sometimes in areas where extensive clearing of rainforest has taken place the *Capparis* trees regenerate from root suckers and the female Caper Whites will then utilise them. At times large migrations of this butterfly can be seen, especially over the eastern half of the continent. Eggs are laid in clusters and mostly the larvae remain grouped together.

Both the **Lemon** and **Common Migrant** butterflies can be seen in very large numbers at times, forming extensive migrations. They are more common in the eastern half of Australia but at times cover most of the mainland. The **Lemon Migrant** usually lays its eggs on *Cassia* trees while the **Common Migrant** uses annual or perennial Senna herbs, the most common being *Senna barclayana* and related species. The larvae and pupae of both species are near enough to identical, only the plant they are feeding on will separate them.

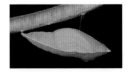

Common Migrant.

Lemon Migrant.

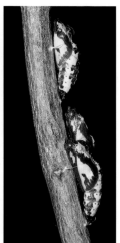

The **Wood White** butterfly is found from about the Atherton Tableland (where it is very scarce) to Adelaide, with sporadic occurrences in the centre and becoming common again in south-west Western Australia. The main host plants are the parasitic shrubs and trees, Quandong and Sandal-wood (*Santalum* species). They also use many species of mistletoe.

It is not known why they are not common at the northern end of their range as there is an abundance of host plants in this area.

The female of the Wood White (*Delias aganippe*), like all butterflies in the *Delias* group, lays her eggs in clusters and the larvae remain together this way, even pupating in groups along branches. The adults are one of the most colourful in this group, outdone only by the spectacular *Delias aruna* from Cape York Peninsula, which is bright orange.

Large migrations of this butterfly pass through Victoria each year and lay many eggs on Olive trees. Why they do this remains a mystery as the Olive tree is not a host plant and all the larvae die. This usually only happens to butterflies that encounter a closely related plant from South America, but the Olive is completely unrelated to our parasitic plants.

The **Glasswing** can be found almost anywhere in mainland Australia but is more common in the north, east and south of the continent. The main host plants for their larvae are native *Passiflora* (passion vines), *Adenia* and *Hybanthus* (Spade Flower). The Spade Flower is a small herb that is very widespread, thus giving this butterfly the ability to breed in very remote regions. They can become very prolific in the top end of Northern Territory and Western Australia when breeding on *Adenia*. This is a large vine with soft foliage and a single plant can support many hundreds of larvae.

The adults live for many months and usually spend the winter/dry season in moist, sheltered areas where there is a good supply of nectar so they can survive without expending too much energy to find flowers.

Female.

Male.

The **Common Eggfly** is found over the eastern half of mainland Australia, extending across to about Broome in the top end. The females are extremely variable and some seasons numerous colour aberrations can be seen. The one illustrated here is somewhat more colourful than the normal form.

The larvae are often found on the weed *Sida rombifolia*, also known as *Sida retusa* or Paddy's Lucerne. A widespread natural host is the small herb Alternanthera, of which there are a number of species. These butterflies will also lay and feed on the common garden plant *Asystasia gangetica*.

Meadow Argus occurs Australia-wide. It prefers open meadow country and usually breeds in areas where there is very short grass and prostrate (ground hugging) herbs. A favoured host plant is Plantago, often called Plantain, but the larvae will also feed on introduced Verbena and garden plants such as Snapdragon (Antirrhinum) and Summer Snapdragon (Angelonia). In suburban gardens the females are content to lay on these plants provided they are growing in the full sun.

Following widespread rains over most of Australia (which does not happen very often, the last period being 1973–74) large migrations of this butterfly are often seen. Usually they fly quite fast and low to the ground but when migrating they tend to move through at between three and ten metres above the ground.

The **Australian Painted Lady** is found over most of Australia, including Tasmania, but is absent from the top end of Northern Territory and Western Australia. The larvae feed on numerous species of plants in the Daisy family (Asteraceae), especially Paper Daisies.

The larvae web leaves together to make a shelter where they hide when not feeding.

Large migrations of this butterfly are often seen following good rains in inland regions. These migrations can be over a front as wide as 500km and last for several weeks, consisting of incalculable numbers.

The **Australian Admiral** can be found anywhere in Australia where its host plants grow. While Stinging Nettle is the main host, the females will also lay on the annual herbs *Parietaria debilis* and *Laportea interrupta*. These small plants look very much like Stinging Nettle but they do not sting. They are usually found in lightly shaded, permanent damp places such as sandstone gorges or the mouth of caves where water seeps. In the dry inland parts of Australia these are the main host plants as Stinging Nettle (*Urtica*) is mostly restricted to higher rainfall regions.

The image on the right shows a clump of *Laportea interrupta* growing in the mouth of a cave in an otherwise very dry area.

In dry areas the adult butterflies semi-hibernate when necessary to await rains that will produce a new generation of these annual plants.

Laportea interrupta.

MOTHS

The number of Moth species outnumbers the number of Butterfly species by 50:1. Because they generally fly at night they are rarely seen unless they are drawn to a light.

Two groups of large moths are quite widespread, they are Hawk Moths and Emperor Moths and you are almost certain to encounter some of these in your garden.

Emperor Gum Moth.

Hawk Moths sit with wings spread and resemble a delta-winged jet plane. Their wings move like hummingbirds and they hover over flowers to feed with their very long proboscis. Most are night-flying but the Bee Hawk Moths and Hummingbird Hawk Moths feed openly by day.

ARE ANY CATERPILLARS DANGEROUS?

A number of moths have caterpillars that can sting or cause a violent itching reaction.

Cup Moth larvae.

Most **Cup Moth** larvae are very colourfully marked, which may make them attractive to children. They are extremely dangerous. Their spines can inflict a serious sting if touched. While there are many different species, they usually are easy to identify because of their colourful markings and bristling spines.

The larvae of the Procession Moth are covered with long hairs which can cause severe itching for some people when they come into contact with them. When moving from one tree to another the larvae form a long line, hence the name. The 'bag' on the tree trunk to the right is formed when the caterpillars gather to moult or change into their pupae. Do not disturb is the best policy. They usually feed on Wattle Trees.

Procession Moth.

PRAYING MANTIDS

Most people have seen or heard of Praying Mantids. They are predators and will eat anything small enough for them to grab and hold. The 'praying' part of the name comes from the position they adopt when waiting for prey. They sit with the front legs raised, ready to strike.

Female Mantid just finished laying a batch of eggs.

Nymph stage of the Garden Mantid. The wings are small and not yet properly formed.

When the female lays eggs they are covered with foam. This foam then sets and forms a rather soft but very effective protective coating for the eggs.

The female in the image on the left has just finished laying. This is a small species of Mantid but you will note the very large front legs with which she catches and holds her prey.

The image on the left is an adult Garden Mantid. When the nymph moults for the last time the wings are complete and it is then an adult.

The eyes are on stalks and this gives this insect an almost 360-degree view of its surroundings. This means it can see prey in any direction and a predator of the Mantid has no chance of sneaking up on it.

Mantids are found over most of Australia. In the cooler regions the nymphs take all year to mature but in warmer northern regions they may have two broods in a season.

Hundreds of tiny Mantids cascade down from the egg case when they hatch and quickly disperse amongst the foliage.

Adult Garden Mantid.

BEES AND WASPS

There are over 1,500 species of native bees in Australia and the majority of gardeners are not aware of most of them. The best-known ones are in the stingless group that are social and build hives in hollow branches and even in the brick wall of a house, entering through the small ventilation gaps between some of the bricks.

There are about ten species of these stingless bees and all the remainder are solitary. Each female of these solitary species makes her own nest-burrow in the ground or in dead branches or stumps, but some species will often dig burrows side by side and form a colony of individuals. They usually dig in sandy soil, so to entice these to breed you need a few small piles of sand in the garden, and preferably in the full sun.

Neon Cuckoo Bee.

Like most birds in the cuckoo family, **Cuckoo Bee** females lay their eggs in the nests of other species of bees, usually killing and eating the larvae of the host bee. The Neon Cuckoo Bee is a striking insect.

Cuckoo Bee.

Leafcutter Bee.

This **Cuckoo Bee** lays her eggs in the nest of Leafcutter Bees that her markings closely resemble. Even though Cuckoo Bees do not gather pollen they feed on nectar so contribute to the pollination of many flowers.

Female **Leafcutter Bees** cut circular pieces out of leaves which are taken to the burrow, rolled up and used to house the eggs.

This rather wasp-like bee belongs to the Halictid Bee group and has no common name. This group of bees nests in burrows in the ground or sometimes in rotten wood. At times multiple females will use the same area but each cares for her own eggs.

Halictid Bees are important pollinators of our native plants, as are most of our other bee species. Males do not nest but cluster together at night.

Mellitidia tomentifera.

Blue-banded Bees are found in all mainland states and are very important pollinators of native plants. Some literature says that they favour blue or mauve flowers but in our garden I have found that they visit flowers with a very wide range of colours, including yellow, red and white.

They are know as Buzz Pollinators, their wings move very rapidly and create quite a down draft. Some of our native flowers require the flower to be vibrated to release the pollen and their fertilisation can only be achieved by this type of bee. There are other Buzz Pollinators amongst our native bees.

The females nest in the ground, often in cool protected areas such as underneath overhangs and houses. The males rest and sleep by clamping their jaws onto a twig or leaf.

Blue-banded Bees.

This striped native bee is gathering pollen while a bee from the hive of one of our social stingless bees is waiting its turn.

All our solitary native bees can sting but none are aggressive and you will not get stung unless you try to hold one in your hand.

When is a bee not a bee? That's easy, when it is a wasp. Many wasps take nectar so it is not always a good idea to assume if it is on a flower then it is a bee. Most wasps are the familiar wasp shape and colours but some look rather like bees.

This **Sand Wasp** on the right is just entering its burrow, which is under a leaf. This species forms large colonies and several hundred individuals make burrows near each other. They fly very fast and their behaviour resembles that of some of our native bees.

Flower Wasps pollinate flowers like bees. The female digs through the soil looking for grubs in which she lays her eggs.

Some females are wingless and resemble large ants.

Sand Wasp.

Hairy Flower Wasp.

Yellow Hairy Flower Wasp.

93

A very important group of wasps for the control of pest moth species are the parasitic Ichneumon Wasps. These control a wide range of moths, wasps and beetles by injecting their eggs into the larvae and pupae. If you see them flying low over the lawn they are searching for Lawn Grubs, which are the larvae of a small moth.

Ichneumon Wasps have a long egg-laying device (ovipositor) with which they inject their eggs into a victim. Sometimes the ovipositor is longer than the body.

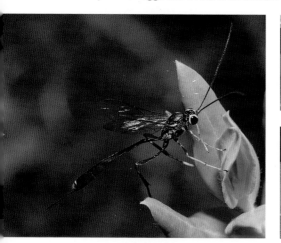

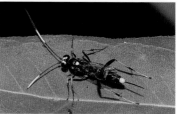

Ichneumon Wasp.

Most wasps look like the two images above. There are numerous species in Australia, some quite passive and others extremely aggressive. Many people who have travelled to the tip of Cape York have a horror story to tell about an attack by wasps. Some wasps build large nests (Paper Wasps), some just small papery nests, some make nests out of mud, while others burrow into the ground.

BEETLES

There are about 30,000 species of beetles in Australia and only about 20,000 of these have been named so far. They eat a wide range of food, including fruit, leaves, bark, wood, fungi, dead animals and even other insects. The majority fly at night but the **Flower Beetles** feed openly during the day and are some of the easiest to observe. Below are a few of these.

Green Chafer Beetle.

Velvet Flower Chafer.

Spotted Flower Chafer.

Green Flower Scarab.

Small Nectar Scarab.

Fiddler Beetle.

95

Click Beetles.

As children we used to find **Click Beetles** a great source of amusement. If you place one on its back it will give a violent kick that shoots it up into the air. It usually lands right-side up, if not it tries again. Their powerful kick can catapult them up to 30cm into the air. If held in your hand the challenge was to see who could hold on without getting a fright and letting it go.

The larvae are called wireworms and usually eat roots, but they are not considered a pest in the garden.

Long-horned Beetles usually chew into the branch or trunk of a tree to lay their eggs. The larvae feed on wood, mostly dead but sometimes not. Some species ring-bark a branch to kill it then lay their eggs on the part that will die, so creating their own dead branch. They have very strong jaws and large ones can inflict a wound if held in the hand.

Leaf Beetles look like Ladybirds but eat leaves and can be a pest in the garden.

Tiger Longicorn Beetle.

Longicorn Beetle.   *Leaf Beetle.*

Lycid Beetles have very distinct antennae that look rather like a saw blade. The adults mostly feed on nectar but there are a few that do not eat at all, feeding only as larvae.

Their typical orange- or red-and-black colours warn potential predators that they are not good to eat.

Lycid Beetle.

Yellow-shouldered Ladybird.

Many **Ladybirds** like the Yellow-shouldered Ladybird above feed on aphids and other small insects. A lot of species are red or orange with black spots and most are very beneficial to the garden as they control aphids, mealybugs and scale insects.

The larvae of these beetles also eat aphids and scale insects, but usually only the very small ones.

The bright yellow-and-black Ladybird on the bottom left eats fungus, rather than insects. This species is also beneficial to the garden as it feeds on the powdery fungus that often damages leaves of plants.

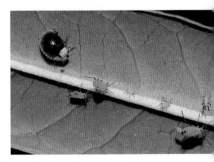

Yellow-shouldered Ladybird lining up a meal of aphids.

Fungus-eating Ladybird.

CICADAS

The drone of Cicadas is the sound of the Australian summer. We have about 200 species and they are found in most habitats. Adults have a fairly short lifespan of only a few weeks, but the nymph stage develops under ground and may take seven or more years to mature. After the first heavy rains of summer the empty nymph cases can be found attached to plants where the adult has emerged. The nymph stage feeds on roots while the adult sucks sap.

Only the males call and as they often call in unison they create a noise that can be uncomfortably loud. The Bladder Cicadas (Green Grocers) call in the evening with an ear-splitting chorus.

They are difficult to identify from books as the illustrations are a top view of a carefully set out specimen.

Cicada – nymph case.

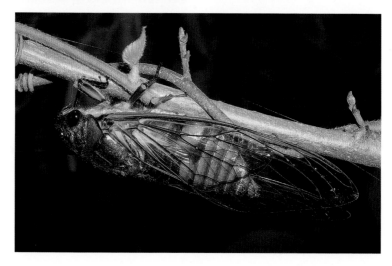

FLIES

Flies are heavily under-rated as pollinators. Numerous flowers of rainforest plants that I have photographed have flies on them, often in fairly large numbers. The following are just a few of the types you may find in the garden. Some of them are rather wild and woolly characters. There are about 20,000 species of flies in Australia.

Tachinid Flies.

Tachinid Flies are parasites. The females lay their eggs on butterfly or moth larvae. When the egg hatches the maggot bores into the larva. It does not usually mature until the pupa is formed, then a fly instead of a butterfly emerges.

Blowflies are a large and diverse group. Many have bright metallic colours and strong bristles. Adults mostly feed on nectar and the maggots on carrion or dung, thus aiding in decomposition.

If you carefully observe the flowers in your garden you will encounter numerous species of flies. They are very difficult to identify and the Queensland Museum has told me that they really need an actual specimen, rather than an image, and even then they might be able to place them in a particular family only. Below are just a few more images to show the infinite variety.

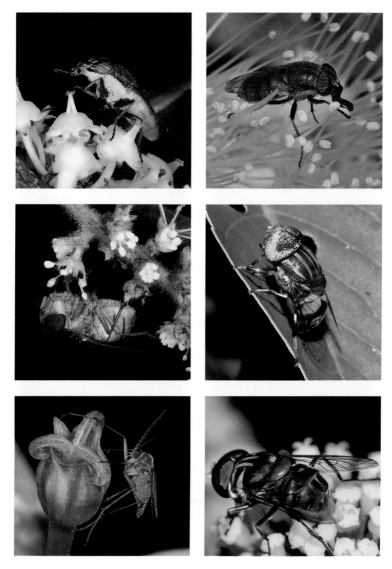

HOVER FLIES

Hover Flies, as the name suggests, move their wings at great speed, enabling them to hover or move very rapidly in any direction. The adults feed on nectar and help to pollinate many flowers. The maggot-like larvae are beneficial to gardeners as they feed on aphids, thrips and small caterpillars.

Adult Hover Fly taking nectar from a Xanthostemon flower.

When hovering the wing-movements are so fast they are invisible to the camera.

Many Hover Flies have body markings that resemble wasps and these have some effect in deterring predators. This is known as Batesian mimicry, after the English naturalist Henry Walter Bates who first observed this phenomenon in the insect world.

ROBBER FLIES

Robber Flies are predators and attack their prey on the wing. They then land on a plant and proceed to suck their victim dry. Sharp spines on their legs help them to hold their prey. To aid digestion, venom is injected into the prey.

The female lays her eggs in soil or rotting wood and the resulting larvae are also predators, feeding on any soft-bodied insect they can catch.

Robber Fly ready to attack.

Having caught a small blue Butterfly, this Robber Fly proceeds to feast on the kill.

BUGS

Bugs are fairly easy to recognise: they are usually flat on top and have a strong sucking device that is used to penetrate other insects or plants. To deter predators many have stink glands that release a foul-smelling chemical, while many can inject venom to paralyse prey. Because of this combination of the stink glands and the venom, caution should be observed and it is a good idea not to handle them. I was stung in the ear by a small green leaf bug and the pain was excruciating.

Some bugs suck nectar as well as sap and the blood of other insects. Sap-sucking species often leave a bacteria behind that kills the soft stem of the plant they are sucking and therefore they are a pest in plant nurseries and gardens.

While taking nectar from flowers this bug decided some beetle blood would be a good addition to its diet.

These small bugs are commonly seen in our garden sucking nectar from a number of different flowers.

This common Green Leaf Bug can be a pest in the vegetable garden and they can pack a powerful sting. They also attack other pest insects and therefore can do some good in the garden.

Some species huddle together in the juvenile stages when they are changing their skins and also when hibernating during the winter. The females of a few species actually look after their small young, which is unusual in the insect world.

Green Stink Bug.

The **Green Stink Bug** feeds on a wide range of plants and can be a pest in the garden on tomatoes and various fruit trees. As the name suggests they release a powerful-smelling chemical when attacked.

Below are some colourful species that display the usual warning colours of toxic or dangerous insects.

STICK AND LEAF INSECTS

Leaf and Stick Insects belong to a group called Phasmids. There are about 150 species in Australia and the largest is the Titan Stick Insect which can grow to 25cm long. The largest Stick Insects usually eat Eucalyptus trees but many are not at all fussy about a particular foliage.

Male.

Female.

This **Spiny Leaf Insect** feeds on a wide range of plants and is probably the largest of our Leaf Insects. The top image is a male and on the left is the female. Females do not have functional wings and so are usually restricted to the tree first found by the tiny ant-like hatchlings.

The eggs are not laid on a tree, rather they are flung out in all directions and take a year or two to hatch. This is rather a haphazard way of laying, but because large numbers of eggs are laid they manage to survive well.

If treated roughly they can release a rather unpleasant-smelling chemical.

WEEVILS

Weevils are a distinctive group of insects that have a long snout, hard shell and very strong legs with sharp claws. When disturbed they often latch onto a plant with these claws and are very difficult to dislodge. They don't do much damage to plants and some tiny species actually pollinate a number of native plants in the Custard Apple family.

Weevils are part of the beetle group of insects. The adults eat plant material such as leaves, bark or dead wood.

The sharp claws can be seen on the individual in the images on the right and centre right. This one was on a fruit on the ground but I don't think it would normally come to the ground to feed. It probably dropped to the ground with the ripe fruit.

Straight-snouted Weevil.   *A Weevil hanging on tight.*

DRAGONFLIES, DAMSELFLIES AND LACEWINGS

Dragonflies and Damselflies lay their eggs in water and their nymph stage preys on aquatic insects, tadpoles and small fish. The adults are also predators. Dragonflies attack on the wing while Damselflies usually eat easier-to-catch food like aphids.

Lacewings are not related to Dragonflies or Damselflies, but because of their superficial resemblance they have been included here. Lacewings are also predators in the larva and adult stages. Like Butterflies they have a four-stage lifecycle: egg, larva, pupa and adult. The larvae often web the bodies of their victims on their back to act as camouflage, it makes them look like a bit of debris on a plant.

Adult Dragonfly.

Dragonfly nymph.

Dragonflies rest with their wings outspread and are usually larger than Damselflies. The nymph in the above image is covered in mud from burrowing around on the bottom of a pond.

Damselflies usually rest with their wings held back beside their body and their eyes are more widely separated than those of Dragonflies.

Common Bluetail Damselfly.

Lacewings usually rest with their wings in a tent-like position, and unlike either Dragonflies or Damselflies they have long antennae. Their eggs are usually laid on long stalks and placed in rows along a branch or leaf.

Blue-eyed Lacewing.

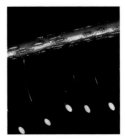

Lacewing eggs.

107

GRASSHOPPERS, CRICKETS AND KATYDIDS

Members of this group have a three-stage lifecycle: egg, nymph and adult. The nymph stage looks very similar to the adult but is wingless. There are about 3,000 species in this group in Australia.

Newly emerged adult.

Wings now completely dry.

Grasshoppers are vegetarians and mostly eat grass, but many of them will take other plant life and can cause problems in the garden or in commercial crops if their numbers are large enough.

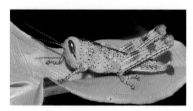

Grasshopper nymph stage.

When the nymph sheds its skin for the last time the adult emerges and the wings expand in a similar fashion to those of a butterfly. The one on the top left has just emerged and is drying its wings, on the right is the same grasshopper after the wings have dried and it is ready to fly.

The image on the bottom right shows all that remains of the nymph stage. The adult's wings were compressed and folded to fit into the small area of the nymph's wing case.

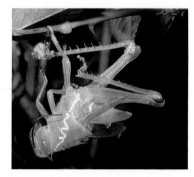

Discarded skin of the nymph.

Katydids look similar to grasshoppers but the adults usually have long antennae and long pointed wings when folded. They are mostly foliage feeders although a few are predatory on other insects.

They usually have high-pitched calls and can be very annoying if they get inside your house. Other species produce calls beyond the range of human hearing.

Some species can adapt their colour to match the plant on which they are feeding but the nymph on the right has certainly got it wrong. There were no pink leaves on the plant it was eating.

Katydid nymph stage.

Adult Katydid.

As well as long antennae, Katydids often have very long hind-legs which enable them to launch well into the air to take flight or to escape predators. The majority of them are nocturnal although you may sometimes find them feeding on plants openly during the day.

Adult Katydid.

Crickets are active by night, many of them emitting the familiar and rather monotonous call that most people are aware of.

Tree Crickets have very long antennae, usually several times the length of their body. They are mostly omnivorous (they will eat anything) and I am sure the ones that feed on other insects use these huge antennae to detect prey. When we had our butterfly farm they were a major pest in the butterfly cage. I observed one sitting motionless with antennae hanging down, then it went straight to a caterpillar and attacked it.

They usually rest in rolled leaves for the day and move out at night to feed. The one on the left is a nymph and the one above is an adult.

They have powerful jaws and a full grown one can inflict a bite that will draw blood if you hold it.

The nymph in the image on the left shows the enormous length of their antennae, many times that of the body.

The sound of the common Chirping Field Cricket is known to most people because it is so loud. Even though you might hear them almost every night during the summer they are rarely seen. Sometimes one that is attracted to a light gets inside the house and is seen hopping along the floor. They occur Australia-wide and feed on decaying matter, both vegetable and animal.

SPIDERS

Spiders are not insects; they belong to a class called Arachnida. Arachnids have four pairs of legs whereas insects have only three pairs. Ticks belong to the same class as spiders.

All spiders have venom that they use to kill or immobilize their prey and help in the digestion of their victims. Spiders do not have chewing devices and take all their nourishment as liquid. Their venom helps break down their prey and they often roll the victim up in silk and when sufficiently liquid they suck what they can from them. Even though they all have venom, most are not considered dangerous to humans. As with snakes, if you are not familiar with them it is best to take care to avoid being bitten.

Garden Orb-weaver.

The **Garden Orb-weaver** is a very common spider that you may encounter. Usually they will remove their web in the morning and seek shelter in folded leaves for the day, rebuilding the web each night. Like most spiders, close up they look quite scary.

Often more common inside the house or a shed than in the garden is the **Daddy Long-legs**. While their web and the remains of their prey create a bit of a mess, they do quite a good job of cleaning up small insects that invade houses and sheds.

Daddy Long-legs.

Golden Orb-weaver.

One of the most spectacular of all the web-building spiders is the **Golden Orb-weaver**. The fully grown females build huge webs that are capable of capturing large moths and even small birds. I once witnessed a Double-barred Finch get caught and in less than a minute it was dead. The spider raced down, grabbed it and bit it on the back of the neck.

The large ground-dwelling Whistling or Barking Spiders are sometimes called Bird-eating Spiders, probably because they are related to the South American Tarantula Spiders, but the Golden Orb-weaver is probably the only real bird-eating spider in Australia.

The tiny male in the top right corner of the image has been highlighted so it can be easily seen.

The female usually goes down to the ground at the beginning of winter, lays her eggs in a golden sack of silk, and dies.

Net-casting Spider.

Net-casting Spiders catch their prey in a most unusual manner. They weave a net and use it like a fisherman uses a cast-net to trap their quarry. When the spider is hunting it holds the net with four legs, stretching it into a square, and when a suitable victim is close enough it thrusts the net down over it, wraps it up and eats it as other spiders do.

The spider in the image above has positioned itself just the correct distance from the Staghorn fern leaf so that it can reach any prey with the net.

Net-casting Spiders do not build a permanent web, rather they make a very basic web to support themselves and the net, moving on to another location if necessary to find food. Sometimes they eat the web from the net to recycle it and other times they leave the old net behind and build a new one when they have relocated. They feed on any insect that is small enough to cope with.

Common Brown Huntsman.   *Tree Huntsman.*

Huntsman Spiders can grow very large and often enter houses. Even though they look quite ferocious they are reluctant to bite humans and prefer to run away. If they reside in your house or garage they will be helping to clean up some pests.

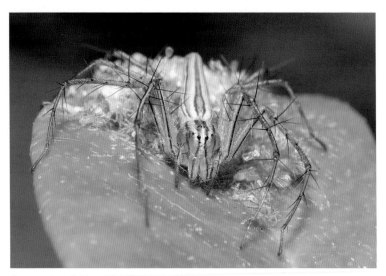

Common Lynx Spider with babies.

Lynx Spiders are active hunters. Rather than build a web they stalk their prey and pounce on them like a lynx.

Because they use their keen eyesight to identify prey they operate by day, jumping and running over foliage. The female guards her eggs until they hatch, reducing the chance of them being eaten.

Garden Jumping Spider.

Jumping Spiders can be found almost anywhere. They have even better eyesight than the Lynx Spiders, with clear vision for 360 degrees. Even though they are only small, mostly less than 1cm in length, they are capable of catching prey quite a bit larger than themselves.

The two large front eyes are actually capable of zooming in on an object, with a zoom range of from 60 to 10 degrees, rather like a pair of zoom binoculars. They are capable of identifying their prey from at least 30cm.

With such good eyesight they only hunt during the day. They do not use a web to catch their prey but at night they create a small web shelter to hide in and the female lays her eggs in this type of shelter.

Some species are highly colourful and as they are not dangerous to humans they can make an interesting study in the garden. Like butterfly and moth caterpillars they leave a silken thread wherever they go, and this can be used as a life support if they leap off a plant to escape a predator.

Green Jumping Spider.

115

Barking Spider beside its burrow.

Barking Spiders are the largest spiders found in Australia. They are sometimes also called Whistling Spiders, Australian Tarantulas, or Bird-eating Spiders, although I doubt if they ever actually eat any birds.

They usually create a web-lined burrow that starts under a log or rock. If you lift whatever they are hiding under they will dart into the burrow. The sack of eggs on the bottom right was photographed after the female tried to drag it into the burrow but it got stuck in the entrance.

There are quite a number of different species, belonging to two groups, but they all look fairly similar, mostly being hairy and always having two finger-like spinnerets at the end of their body.

They are generally found in the warmer parts of Australia, in rainforest, open forest and desert. Some of the larger species are farmed and sold as pets. Care needs to be taken as their bite can be fatal to cats and dogs but it is less of a problem to humans. They can grow up to 6cm long with a leg-span of 16cm, and 1cm-long fangs.

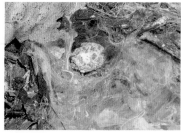

Eggs.

WHAT GARDEN WILDLIFE CAN BE SEEN AT NIGHT?

POSSUMS, GLIDERS, WALLABIES AND FLYING-FOXES are the main mammals that are active during the night, and with a good spotlight these can frequently be observed in gardens. Nocturnal birds such as Owls will sometimes be sighted but these are fairly elusive. While many birds can be seen during the day it is surprising how few can be found sleeping at night. You may think that birds go high up into the trees to sleep but many of them sleep low down on small branches. This gives them protection from winds and they are easily alerted if a predator such as a snake crawls onto the branch. The following are a few images of sleeping birds from our garden. Be careful not to disturb them!

Many birds sleep like the two below, tucking their head under their wing and fluffing up their feathers. At times it is difficult to tell what species they are.

Juvenile male Figbird.

Eastern Yellow Robin.

Peaceful Doves huddle together in pairs.

Dollarbirds tend to sleep higher up than many other species.

117

HOW DO I ATTRACT MORE WILDLIFE TO MY GARDEN?

THERE IS ONE VERY SIMPLE RULE to follow: the more native plants you have in your garden the more wildlife you will attract. A garden that contains only introduced plants, even a large one, will have very few examples of wildlife and is almost guaranteed to attract pest birds such as mynas and sparrows.

The size of your block will determine how you go about attracting wildlife. It is unfortunate that over the years the average suburban blocks have been shrinking. Back in the 1950s blocks were 800–1,000sq m, now some are as small as 200sq m. The last ten years has seen a rapid shrinking in size. Anyone that really wants to have a large wildlife garden should be looking for a rural residential block far enough out of town so as not to be swallowed up too soon. My wife and I live on such a block. About 40 years ago the estate was formed and consisted of five-acre (roughly two-hectare) blocks. The local council has now allowed the blocks to be split in two. This is still quite a large block and as many people that purchase 5 acres end up not really doing much with them, they become weed infested and a fire hazard. A more manageable size for most people is half to one acre. Quite a large estate was set up adjoining ours with these smaller sized blocks and the planting of trees was encouraged by the developer who issued a voucher for 20 free trees from a local native plant nursery. When these plants grew well people were then enthused to buy more plants and the whole development is now a great wildlife area. Many people have decided not to fence and this allows the wallabies and bettongs to move freely through the blocks.

WHAT TO DO

First of all it is best to know what **not** to do. Individual trees should not be planted in the lawn. There are several problems with this, mainly the plants are competing with the lawn, they do not have enough loose soil to grow rapidly and they offer little in the form of habitat.

All plants should be in beds. Even if the bed has only about five or six plants this will provide shelter as the plants merge and the undisturbed leaf litter on the ground is an excellent habitat for lizards and many insects.

When you decide where a bed should be, mark it out, remove the grass, or spray to kill it, then dig up the entire area of the bed. Deep cultivation will provide the best results but this is not always practical. In our garden we used a D4 bulldozer with rippers. The feeder roots of a tree are only in the first 20–30cm of soil so this is the most important depth to cultivate. You may be able to hire a walk-behind-rotary-hoe locally and this will be easier than digging by hand. An alternative is to hire a Bobcat and get the operator to dig with a 45cm bucket. All that is needed is to dig with the bucket then tip it so the soil falls back into the hole. It will be partly overturned so this is effectively cultivated. The purpose of cultivation is to loosen and aerate the soil. The bed should then be mulched with any locally available material. Local councils often have free mulch from tree prunings available at the dump.

The following mulches in order of value for money can be considered:

Peanut shell. This is by far the best mulch when it is available from a shelling factory. It lasts a long time (up to five years in our climate), is very clean, and the fine parts break down fairly quickly, greatly enriching the soil. On our block we used many hundreds of cubic metres of this mulch. We were lucky as we got it cheaply (paying only for the cartage) before everyone found the real value of it.

Wood-chip from tree prunings. This is similar to peanut shell in performance although it usually only lasts up to three years. If it has been stored for a year or more the nutrient value is not as high, but it still fulfils the basic requirements.

Hay. This is easy to spread, especially when it comes in round bales, but it breaks down very quickly, usually only lasting for one year. This means the bed will have to be re-done at least once more before the leaf drop from the trees can supply enough cover. The advantage is that organic material is added to the soil quite quickly.

Lawn clippings. One problem with this mulch is that it can sometimes be too fine and may reduce air-flow and the absorption of water. It is absurd though to throw lawn clippings in the bin as this is a waste of a good resource.

The purpose of mulch is to prevent water loss from the soil by evaporation, keep the soil cool and prevent weeds from germinating. **Never** mix the mulch into the soil. Doing this enables the moisture to escape quickly and it is possible nutrients may be tied up with Nitrogen draw-down as bacteria breaks down the mulch. Some books claim putting green (fresh) mulch on a bed causes this but I have been mulching garden beds for at least 40 years and my observations have shown that the only result of green mulch is a flush of new growth from the plants as they absorb the released nutrients. If green mulch is applied too thickly (30cm deep or more) it is possible the composting action may produce too much heat and damage roots.

An area of our garden in November 1986, deep ripped and heavily mulched with peanut shell, ready for planting in January 1987 (during the wet season).

A nice mixed bed is being established on this property. When the new addition of trees and shrubs in front are established this will be a very effective wildlife habitat and privacy screen.

This small bed has only six plants but is a great way to provide nectar with a mix of either Callistemons or Grevilleas. Growing them in the full sun ensures plenty of flowers most of the year.

The well-established garden bed on the left is 30 years old. Our house is just behind it, but from the lawn it cannot be seen.

Once a garden bed is ten or more years old you may need to do some lopping and pruning to keep some plants small if they are near a building.

In this rural residential estate landowners were encouraged to plant trees and it is now a haven for many species of wildlife. This is the view down just one street. Not everyone planted native plants but most did.

The planting on the right could have been better if it had not been mounded. The problem with planting trees on mounds is that in six or eight years time the mound is completely packed with roots and very little moisture can penetrate. A lot of the feeder roots of the plants are in this mound and the trees will often be very stressed.

You should always dig up the existing ground rather than mound, so the moisture content will be evenly spread.

Mounds should only be considered if it is to create a noise barrier near a highway, and then the mound should be narrow and about three metres high with the trees planted at the base on each side. Wider mounds can be used if in swampy or very high rainfall areas to prevent waterlogging of the plants or to grow plants from a drier area.

121

SHOULD FOOD BE PLACED OUT TO ATTRACT WILDLIFE?

IF YOU LOOK AT ANY government website you will get the very strong message: 'Don't feed the wildlife'. If you talk to bird enthusiasts you will find that large numbers of people feed birds. In most overseas countries providing food for wild birds is a huge industry.

In spite of all the warnings on Australian websites urging householders not to feed wild birds the ratio of people that do so is the same as in other countries where it is 'good' and 'kind'.

I do not think wild mammals should be given food as many are strongly territorial and crowding together can cause many problems. You should simply provide a suitable habitat and let nature take its course.

I have seen an instance of wallabies being fed and they built up to very large numbers causing huge problems for neighbours, virtually destroying their gardens.

Some bird species should not be encouraged by feeding and these include:

Currawongs. These are very aggressive and usually move around to find food at different times of the year. If they stay in the one place they can put pressure on many other bird species.

Brush-turkeys. Their numbers can build up to ridiculous levels. One place I saw that used to feed them had 130 birds coming each day.

Noisy Miners. These are very aggressive birds and if their numbers build up in an area they hunt out many small birds.

Butcherbirds. Because they are predators it is reasoned that unusual numbers of them can have a detrimental effect on other birds. I have no knowledge of this and it could be a theoretical problem. As they are strongly territorial you may still only have one pair or family.

Kookaburras. The same reasons as for Butcherbirds are given but I know of one instance where they are fed and only the local pair and their offspring come for food.

The fact is that surveys have shown that between 40-80 per cent of Australian householders spend money on food trying to attract birds to their backyards. The one thing to remember is, if you are going to feed the wild birds, feed them good quality food.

At 8am and 4pm each day the Currumbin Wildlife Sanctuary feeds thousands of wild lorikeets as a tourist attraction. They have been doing this since 1947 and I have never heard of any major problems. When we lived at Mt Tamborine, in the Gold Coast hinterland, about half an hour before feeding time at Currumbin, flocks of lorikeets would gather and head for the Gold Coast. I can only assume that they feed the birds with properly balanced nutrition.

Darryl Jones, an urban ecologist at Griffith University, is currently writing a book on bird feeding. You can search the Web for various articles that he has written on the subject.

Australian King-parrot and Red-browed Finch sharing some seed.

Pale-headed Rosella at feeder.

ARE NEST BOXES AND HOLLOWS USEFUL?

IN THE CITIES NEST BOXES can be of great benefit to types of wildlife which use that sort of shelter as there are very few old trees that provide natural hollows. It is important to have the nest boxes the correct size for the creature you are trying to encourage. Brushtail Possums will invade boxes if they have an opening that they can squeeze through.

Boxes can be completely artificial or made from natural hollow branches and set up in a suitable location. Marine or industrial ply should be used so it will not fall apart and the outside should be painted with a good external paint such as the type made for fences.

The following illustrations by Lloyd Nielsen show some possible nest boxes, some wholly man-made and some adapted from hollow branches.

Owl nest box positioned in a tree.

Dove box.

Parrot box.

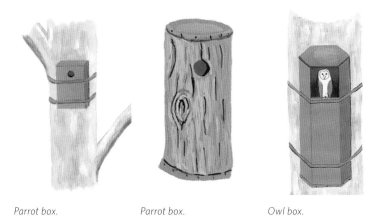

Parrot box.   Parrot box.   Owl box.

Parrot box.   Swallow ledge.

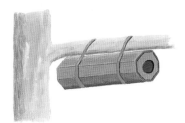

Owl box.

Nest boxes are only part of the solution – they are of little use if your garden does not contain a good range of native plants to provide habitat and a food supply.

Small parrot boxes are also suitable for gliders.

Below are some suggested measurements for nest boxes to suit various birds. It is important to match the entrance size to that of the particular bird so that larger species cannot enter the boxes intended for smaller species such as parrots.

Bird	Height	Width	Depth	Entrance	Mount
Cockatoo, Sulphur-crested	40–100	35	35	15	V
Corella, Little	30–40	30	30	15	V
Corella, Long-billed	30–40	35	35	15	V
Duck, Australian Wood	30–50	25	25	15	V
Duck, Pacific Black	30	35	35	15	H
Galah	60	20	20	12	V
Kookaburra sp.	50	25	25	13	H
Lorikeet, Rainbow	30	12	12	6	H
Lorikeet, Little	20	10	10	3	H
Lorikeet, Musk	25	15	15	4	H
Lorikeet, Purple-crowned	20	10	10	3	H
Owl, Barn	100	50	50	50 (open)	V
Owl, Boobook	30–60	30	30	15	V
Owlet-nightjar, Australian	30	15	15	8	V
Pardalote, Striated	40–50	8	8	4	H
Rosella sp.	75–100	20	20	8	V/H
Shrike-thrush, Grey	20–30	15–20	15–20	15 (open)	V
Swallow, Welcome		13	13	Platform	H
Teal, Chestnut	30–60	20–40	20–40	12	V
Teal, Grey	30–60	20–40	20–40	12	V
Treecreeper sp.	40	9–15	9–15	5–7	V

All measurements in cm. V (vertical) H (horizontal).

Hollows only form on very old trees and in most built-up areas none of these exist or they are very few and far between. No nest box will suit all so you need at least several different sizes. There are commercial suppliers so if you don't want to make the boxes yourself just search the Web and you will find several suppliers of them.

If making your own, ensure that the inside is not smooth so the birds or possums/gliders can easily climb in and out. It is best if the box is positioned with the entrance facing away from the prevailing winds and an overhang is provided to prevent most rain from entering.

It is a good idea to have an inspection door on one side at the bottom so you can inspect and clean out if necessary. This is handy to get rid of pest species like sparrows, starlings and mynas.

Honey bees have been know to take over a nest box; if you don't want to keep these, look for a local bee-keeper to help you move them.

When mounting the box be sure not to completely encircle the tree with the metal strip. You may need to loosen the nails every few years to prevent the bark from growing over the mounting strips.

Trees that have broken branches that hollow out are essential nesting sites for possums, gliders and numerous birds, especially parrots and owls.

ATTRACTING BIRDS TO THE GARDEN

BIRDS CAN BE DIVIDED up into a number of groups according to their diets, but it is not cut and dried as many species bridge different categories.

Nectar-/pollen-feeders. Honeyeaters and Lorikeets are the main birds in this group but they sometimes take fruit and so are not restricted to feeding only on nectar. The majority of Honeyeaters feed their young on insects as does the Figbird. Insects are a source of high protein which is essential for fast-growing young birds. So you can see that simply supplying nectar is not enough – if the birds are to breed in your garden they need a wide range of food and suitable places to build their nests, away from the nectar and fruit supplies.

Insect-eaters. These range from tiny birds like the Fairy Gerygone to the Australian Magpie and even larger. This is probably the largest group of all, especially when you include the Honeyeaters and others that take insects from time to time or feed their young on them. If you are going to attract a wide range of insects, then you need an even wider range of native plants.

Seed-eaters. Included in this group are Finches, Pigeons and Parrots, but like other groups there is no fine line dividing the species. Some birds will eat both seeds and fruit and even Lorikeets, which are mostly nectar-feeders, will call in to a seed tray and happily feed there.

Fruit-eaters. Birds that eat fruit come from a wide range of families and include Pigeons, Cuckoos and even the tiny Mistletoebird. Casual observers often think Sulphur-crested Cockatoos eat fruit but what they are actually doing is ripping open the fruit to get to the seed. They are so smart that with the fruit of the Davidson's Plum, which usually only has one good seed, they can tell which side the good seed is and never open the fruit on the wrong side.

Bird Baths are the most essential part of a bird friendly garden. These provide water to drink as well as for bathing. Birds enjoy bathing, and the whole family can get enjoyment from watching the various antics of different species as they bathe. Some dive in and out in the blink of an eye, while others approach it very cautiously and some splash water all over the place.

The best approach is to have at least two containers, one shallow and one much deeper. In our garden we have the shallow one on top and when it fills automatically from the watering system it overflows into the deeper one. You can buy a commercial one or make your own. I used the lid of a rubbish bin as a mould to make a concrete one. The deeper one is a commercial one made of concrete but resin ones are quite suitable. Glossy plastic ones are of little use as the birds cannot get a grip on them with their feet.

A full house.

129

Permanent water above ground is the perfect place for mosquitoes to breed, especially the Dengue fever carrier, so it is essential to empty them out once a week. You will then have no problem in this regard. If a lot of birds use the bath every day you may need to change the water several times a week to keep it clean and prevent too much algal growth.

Placement of the baths is quite important. If they are out in the open exposed to the full sun you will be lucky to ever see a bird on them. They should be placed in a protected area with plenty of shelter nearby for the birds to duck in and out of. A place that many birds gather regularly is a target for Goshawks so it is a good idea if the baths are positioned so that they cannot be seen from directly above.

Below are various birds enjoying a bath.

Silvereye.

Rainbow Lorikeet – there's nothing like a good splash.

Spangled Drongo – boy that was good!

Lewin's Honeyeater – ready to dive in again.

Eastern Yellow Robin.

Bridled Honeyeater.

White-throated Honeyeater.

A well-positioned bird bath will be a hive of activity for most of the day. You will notice different species come in at particular times but often during the day there will be quite a variety all bathing and drinking at once. When large numbers of birds are using the facilities you may need to wash the baths out every day.

This plastic bath was almost useless when new as it was very slippery, but with age it has changed and now birds can sit on it without any problem.

The bath on the left is made from an old engine part and a plough disc. This one is more ornamental than useful as it does not hold much water.

131

ATTRACTING FRUIT-EATING BIRDS

Birds that eat fruit include Pigeons, Cuckoos, Figbirds, Silvereyes and Mistletoebirds.

Figs are the number one fruit for this group of birds, however the main problem with fig trees is that they are mostly very large, aggressive plants that should **never** be planted in a suburban garden. Figs have a massive root system that can extend up to 100 metres. There is another problem with figs that most people do not realise. Each species of Fig has a specific wasp that fertilisers it so if they are grown outside of their natural range they will not produce fruit and so are of no use for feeding wildlife. One fairly small fig that can be grown in the northern half of Australia is the **Sandpaper Fig** (*Ficus opposita*).

The **Sandpaper Fig** is a large shrub or small tree with very rough (sandpapery) leaves. The fruit usually turn black when ripe and are quite tasty, so there is no need to let the birds have them all.

To get the maximum amount of fruit this plant needs to be grown in the full sun.

Plants in the Sapindaceae (Lychee) family usually have a fleshy coating (aril) over the seed and many birds find these very tasty. In our garden the Superb Fruit-Dove feeds on *Alectryon connatus* (below). One notable exception is the Tamarind group (*Diploglottis* species). Even though these have edible fruit (for humans) and many people make jam and sauces from their flesh, most birds are not interested in them and rarely use them.

Above is a selection of Psychotrias; all species are suitable and they rarely grow more than four metres high. Even Mistletoebirds feed on these.

Shrubs or small trees that have small berries are the ideal plants to grow in a small to medium-sized garden. One of the best is *Psychotria* of which there are a number of species as well as some hybrids in cultivation.

A plant that is often overlooked as a bird attractant is the Flax Lily (*Dianella*). There are many species and quite a few are in cultivation. They can be grown in most Australian gardens. As well as small birds (including Honeyeaters) eating the fruit, Rosella parrots split open the fruit to get the seed.

The giant Weeping Fig (*Ficus benjamina*) is a fantastic tree for birds. It is suitable only for gardens more than one hectare in size and anywhere in the top half of Australia, from about Mackay northwards. It is very suitable for the dry inland. As well as feeding birds it makes an excellent shade tree.

133

Some native fruits that birds are fond of

Dillenia alata – *suitable for the high rainfall tropical areas.*

Celtis paniculata – *occurs from the Northern Territory to south of Sydney and inland in gorges and along streams.*

Melodorum leichhardtii – *will grow anywhere east of the Great Dividing Range.*

Figs are a great resource but suitable only for large gardens.

Micromelum minutum – *suitable for any frost-free area of eastern and northern Australia.*

Flacourtia *sp. Shipton's Flat – Bush-tucker. Available from many nurseries.*

I see nothing wrong with putting out fresh or over-ripe fruit for birds. This is not really much different from growing a tree that will provide fruit most of the time such as a Fig Tree. The best plan is not to have the fruit always available but to place it out once or twice a day at roughly the same time. This will teach the birds that it is not available all the time and they will spread out when the fruit is eaten.

A female or juvenile Satin Bowerbird enjoying some Pawpaw.

Another bird particularly fond of Pawpaw is the female Victoria's Riflebird.

ATTRACTING INSECT-EATING BIRDS

Insect-eating birds are probably the most useful group to have in the garden as they will help to control many of the pests that are a problem to gardeners.

There are a few flowering plants that attract many insects and when these are in flower insect-eating birds visit them.

Grevillea mimosoides.

Grevillea baileyana *is found in the tropical rainforests of north-eastern Queensland but is extremely hardy and will survive anywhere east of the Great Dividing Range.*

It is interesting to note that the two rainforest Grevilleas of north Queensland do not attract birds, though the southern Grevillea robusta (Silky Oak) attracts swarms of them.

The best way to ensure you have this group of birds in the garden is to plant a range of non-bird-attracting plants in a bed or beds. As well as attracting insects many of these plants will then be used for nesting and sleeping. The more plant species you have, the more insects there will be for birds to eat.

ATTRACTING NECTAR-/POLLEN-FEEDERS

These include Honeyeaters and Lorikeets, but species such as the Spangled Drongo, Silvereye and several others also take nectar from time to time. You will find that the species come and go at different times of the year. In the breeding season numbers will be fairly low as birds pair off and become more territorial. Sometimes large numbers of non-breeding birds, often many of them juvenile, will arrive and stay until they have drained the nectar supply. The Scarlet Honeyeater does this and makes a spectacular sight when in large numbers.

A good start is to plant up a bed of mixed Grevilleas, Melaleucas/Callistemons, Banksias and Hakeas. This bed will need to be in the full sun for these plants to flower well. Botanically speaking Callistemons have vanished, these trees are now called Melaleucas but it will take many years for the change to filter down to most nurseries.

Eucalyptus trees are a very good source of nectar but great care is needed in the selection of species. Large Gum trees should never be planted in suburban gardens as they can be ripped out or broken off in wild storms and do extreme damage to your house or your neighbour's. Some of the compact hybrid varieties are suitable and for those in southern states there is a wide range of small species that can be grown. Consult your local native plant nursery.

Grevilleas are one of the best plants to provide a nectar supply in your garden. Your local nursery will have species and hybrids that are suitable for your particular area.

Gum (Eucalyptus) trees provide an abundant supply of nectar in the wild but be careful in selecting them for your garden as many grow very large.

Melaleucas and Callistemons (now botanically the same thing) are popular in gardens and a wide range is usually available from any nursery. Try to select a variety of species so flowering will occur over a long period. Some are quite large, so again be careful in selecting if you have a small garden.

Banksias are particularly good for honeyeaters but be sure to select the species that are suitable for your area. Don't try to grow southern varieties in the tropics.

I don't recommend providing artificial nectar for this group of birds as it is almost impossible to duplicate the natural nutrients that are found in flowers. Just putting out sugared water is not at all healthy for the birds and putting out a mixture containing honey is illegal. Commercial formulas are available and even these should be used sparingly on wild birds; you will find it is often easier to provide real flowers. The same thing applies to birds as to humans – junk food is no good.

There are of course many other plants that provide suitable nectar, so consult your local nursery and check out other gardens in your district to see what flowers birds are visiting.

ATTRACTING SEED-EATING BIRDS

This group includes Finches, Pigeons and Parrots. Finches often eat insects and sometimes will go into a feeding frenzy when flying ants are emerging.

It is difficult to grow plants especially to produce seed for birds. If you have a large garden with a wide selection of tree species some seed-eating birds will find suitable food but on the whole the success will not be high.

The only way to definitely bring seed-eating birds into the garden is to provide seed on a feeding bench. The most important thing is to supply high-quality grain and a mixed variety, not piles of the same type, such as sunflower seed. Be wary of cheap bird seed as it may be mostly husks with very little actual seed.

There are three basic types of seed-eaters:
• Pigeons and doves swallow the seed whole and grind it up in their gizzard;
• Parrots rip the seed open and extract the kernel;
• Finches grind up the seed in their bill, with bits of seed flying everywhere, and swallow mainly the kernel.

From this you can see that cracked corn is of little use to parrots and finches as they will not obtain what they require. Another consideration is the size of the grain. To provide feed for any species that may drop in you will need a good range of sizes. A lot of the 'wild bird seed' sold in shops does not have enough small seed for finches and a good idea is to buy Budgie seed and add it to the mix. Large pigeons like Bar-shouldered Doves and Bronzewing Pigeons can eat corn but most other species require smaller grain.

This Emerald Dove is getting ready to enjoy a selection of seed.

Gardeners use various different ways of feeding the seed-eating birds. The simplest way of all is just to throw some seed down on a paved or concrete area.

This method can be quite effective and it is certainly easy. There could be a problem if your or a neighbour's cat is not well behaved since the birds at ground-level could be an easy target.

One solution is to make an enclosure with wide mesh and place the seed inside. The mesh needs to be wide enough for any bird species attracted to walk through. This is also useful if you have domestic chickens roaming in the garden. The bird seed will be reserved just for the birds.

If you have Brush-turkeys in your area then this is another reason why feeding birds this way is not suitable. The Brush-turkey is one bird you should never encourage by feeding. Usually the numbers will slowly build up until there are large numbers of them. Even if you have a mesh enclosure they will push their long neck through and if the mesh is not firmly fixed they will push it along until they get to the seed. Most gardeners find this bird a major problem, especially if a male starts to build a mound.

Above is the feeding tray arrangement that we have in our garden for the seed-eaters. Birds that come to eat these seeds are Finches (three types), Bar-shouldered Doves, Peaceful Doves, Emerald Doves and Pale-headed Rosellas.

Below is a group of finches enjoying some assorted grain. It is a good idea to have two or more feeders so there is room for both small and large birds to feed at the same time. This feeder is close to the two main bird baths.

ATTRACTING FROGS TO THE GARDEN

A FROG POND IS A VERY IMPORTANT part of a garden for anyone keen on wildlife. The pond does not have to be very big to be successful but there are a few considerations to take into account.

If you have toads in your area then it may be necessary to screen it to keep them out but you can simply exclude toads from breeding in a pond by positioning it in the shade. We have two small ponds in our garden, both in the shade, and these are very successful. Toads will sit in the ponds at night but they lay their eggs only in the full sun.

This pond is in a pergola beside the house and the water is mostly topped up by the automatic watering system that waters plants on benches above the pond. Sometimes in the very dry parts of the year extra water may need to be added.

The pond above is only 1.8m x 1m x 8cm deep and has a clay base to hold water. The tadpoles sitting on the bottom in this image are those of the Striped Marsh Frog. Sometimes there is not enough natural food in the pond to nourish the tadpoles so we sprinkle a little fish flakes from time to time.

The main thing to watch with any pond is not to let it dry out when it still has tadpoles in it. Some species take many months to mature so you have to keep a good eye on the water level. We have not found toads sitting in the water some nights to be a problem – it does not seem to affect the tadpoles.

Larger pond with fish and water plants.

The above image is of a pond in our fernery. It has a plastic pond-liner base and is approximately 2m in diameter by 30cm deep. The large fish are local rainbows and the small ones exotic platies. These add a bit of interest to the pond and ensure mosquitoes do not breed. These fish no doubt eat some of the frog eggs and small tadpoles, but often half a dozen frogs lay, producing huge numbers of eggs so they cannot possibly all survive. Usually species that produce large numbers of eggs have a very low survival rate.

The water plants are from local creeks and irrigation channels so are in their local climate range. It is important not to use introduced weeds in ponds as during the wet season these may escape and contaminate waterways.

This Striped Marsh Frog is lurking in the pond. During most of the year their plonk plonk call can be heard through the night.

Striped Marsh Frog in process of laying eggs.

Egg-laying complete and ready for hatching.

ATTRACTING BUTTERFLIES
TO THE GARDEN

UNLIKE BIRDS, BUTTERFLIES HAVE very basic requirements. Butterfly larvae require quite specific host plants that they have to eat and the female selects these plants to lay her eggs on. If you have host plants for various butterflies and you live within their natural range, the females will eventually locate these host plants and lay their eggs.

Most adult butterflies feed on nectar and no specific nectar plants are needed, so provided you have some flowers for the adults and host plants for the larvae you will attract butterflies to your garden.

Butterfly larvae (caterpillars) eat leaves so be prepared to have the host plants take on a somewhat eaten look.

Best results are obtained if two or three plants for each species are planted and that they be positioned as far apart as possible. This ensures the maximum number of eggs are laid on them. Plants grouped close together are treated as one plant and most butterflies prefer to spread their eggs over as wide an area as possible. If the plants are stripped of most of their foliage just apply some fertiliser and they will bounce back.

Butterflies prefer nectar plants that have tubular flowers but they will use almost any flowers if needed. The best colours are in the pink, mauve or red colour range. Two of the best plants are Pentas and Buddleia. Pentas flowers all year round but is frost sensitive, Buddleia varieties that flower at different times of the year can be obtained, and are more suited to cooler climates. Flowers grown in the full sun produce the best results.

The brightly coloured Leopard butterfly is restricted to the top end of Northern Territory so if you live in the Darwin region keep an eye our for this little beauty. The larvae feed on the native Flacourtia territoralis *and also introduced* Flacourtia *planted as street trees.*

Butterflies which can be attracted to the garden

To have a chance of attracting a specific butterfly you need to be within about 100km of its natural range.

Butterfly	Range
Cairns Birdwing	Hopevale to Sarina
Richmond Birdwing	Maryborough to the Richmond River
Big Greasy	North-west WA to north NSW
Red-bodied Swallowtail	Cape York to Townsville
Ulysses Swallowtail	Cape York to Byfield
Dingy Swallowtail	Eastern Australia
Orchard Swallowtail	Eastern Australia
Ambrax Swallowtail	Cooktown to Ingham
Capaneus/Canopus Swallowtail	Kimberley to Gove and Cape York to northern NSW
Chequered Swallowtail	Mainland Australia
Four-bar Swordtail	Cape York to Port Macquarie
Five-bar Swordtail	Cape York to Rockhampton
Macleay's Swallowtail	Cape York to Tasmania
Blue Triangle	Cape York to southern NSW
Pale Green Triangle	Kimberley to northern NSW
Green Triangle	Cape York to Townsville
Green Spotted Triangle	Cape York to Rockhampton
Common Crow	Most of mainland Australia
Eastern Brown Crow	Cape York to northern NSW
Two-brand Crow	Cape York to Rockhampton
Wanderer	Most of Australia
Lesser Wanderer	Australia-wide
Orange Tiger	Mataranka to Kununurra
Black-and-white Tiger	Kimberley to central NSW
Blue Tiger	Northern WA to eastern Vic
Cairns Hamadryad	Cape York to Townsville
Swordgrass Brown	Cooktown to Townsville then south Qld to SA

Best Host Plants for the Garden	Lays in
Aristolochia acuminata, A. deltantha	Sun or shade
Aristolochia acuminata, A. praevenosa	Shade, sun
Aristolochia acuminata	Sun
Aristolochia acuminata	Shade
Melicope rubra, M. elleryana	Sun
Citrus	Sun
Citrus, Micromelum	Sun
Citrus, Micromelum	Shade
Citrus, Clausena	Shade, sun
Cullen (Psoralea)	Sun
Melodorum leichhardtii	Sun
Miliusa brahei	Shade, sun
Cryptocarya, Daphnandra, Atherosperma	Shade, sun
Cryptocarya, Litsea	Sun, shade
Melodorum leichhardtii, custard apple	Sun
Miliusa brahei, soursop	Sun
Melodorum leichhardtii, soursop	Shade
Nerium (oleander)	Sun, shade
Trophis scandens	Sun, shade
Marsdenia geminata, M. pleiadenia	Sun, shade
Asclepias curassavica, Gomphocarpus (milkweed)	Sun
Asclepias curassavica, Gomphocarpus (milkweed)	Sun, shade
Sarcostemma esculentum	Shade, sun
Cynanchum carnosum	Shade, sun
Heterostemma, Secamone elliptica	Sun, shade
Parsonsia vines	Shade
Gahnia sieberiana (swordgrass)	Shade

Butterfly	Range
Tailed Emperor	Northern and eastern Australia
Glasswing	Mainland Australia, more common in the north and east
Orange Lacewing	Top end of NT
Red Lacewing	Cape York to Townsville
Cruiser	Cape York to Rockhampton
Australian Vagrant	Cape York to Townsville
Australian Rustic	Cape York to northern NSW
Leopard	North-west NT
Australian Fritillary	Gympie to northern NSW
Orange Aeroplane	Cape York to Rockhampton
Common Aeroplane	Cape York to southern NSW
Australian Leafwing	Cape York to northern NSW
Blue-banded Eggfly	Cape York to Rockhampton
Common Eggfly	Northern and eastern Australia
Danaid Eggfly	Kimberley, top of NT and Cape York to central NSW
Australian Lurcher	Top end of NT and from Cape York to Ingham
Blue Argus	Kimberley to south-east Qld
Meadow Argus	Australia-wide
Brown Soldier	Northern and eastern Australia to south Qld
Australian Painted Lady	Cooktown to Tasmania and west to central WA
Australian Admiral	Australia-wide
White Nymph	Cape York to northern NSW
Common Migrant	Eastern half of Australia
Lemon Migrant	Northern half of Australia and east to Victoria
Orange/Yellow Migrant	Kimberley to central NSW
Small Grass-yellow	Australia-wide
Common Grass-yellow	Northern and eastern Australia to southern NSW

Best Host Plants for the Garden	Lays in
Albizia, Cassia, Acacia plants with true leaves	Sun
Passiflora cinnabarina, Adenia heterophylla	Sun, shade
Adenia heterophylla, A. australis	Shade, sun
Adenia heterophylla	Shade, sun
Adenia heterophylla, native *Passiflora* species	Shade, sun
Homalium circumpinnatum , Xylosma species	Shade, sun
Scolopia braunii, Flacourtia, Xylosma	Sun, shade
Flacourtia, Scolopia braunii	Shade, sun
Viola betonicifolia	Shade, sun
Senna gaudichaudii	Shade, sun
Brachychiton, Celtis	Sun, shade
Asystasia gangetica, Pseuderanthemum variable	Sun, shade
Asystasia gangetica, Pseuderanthemum variable	Sun
Sida rhombifolia, Alternanthera	Sun
Asystasia gangetica, Portulaca oleracea (pigweed)	Sun
Dipteracanthus, Hemigraphis	Sun
Asystasia gangetica	Sun
Verbena rigida, Plantago	Sun, shade
Hygrophylla, Hemigraphis	Sun, shade
Paper daisies	Sun
Stinging nettle	Sun, shade
Pipturus argenteus	Shade, sun
Senna barclayana	Sun, shade
Cassia trees	Sun
Senna auriculata, Senna gaudichaudii	Sun, shade
Senna gaudichaudii	Sun, shade
Breynia	Sun, shade

Butterfly	Range
Chalk White	Eastern Australia to central NSW
Common Pearl-white/Narrow-winged Pearl-white	Northern, eastern and southern Australia
Caper White	Australia-wide
Australian Gull	Northern and eastern Australia south to central NSW
Common Albatross	Kimberley to Victoria
Grey Albatross	Cooktown to Townsville
Jezebels (*Delias* species)	Northern, eastern and southern Australia – scarce in the west
Regent Skipper	Cooktown to central NSW
Green Awl	Cape York to northern NSW
Common Banded Awl	Kimberley to Mackay
Palm Darts	Perth to northern NSW, rarely more than 200km from the coast
Common Moonbeam	Cape York to northern NSW
Black-and-white Tit	Cape York to Bowen
Indigo Flash	Cape York to SE Qld
Cornelian	Cape York to southern NSW
Australian Plane	Cape York to Mackay
Helenita Blue	Cape York to about Townsville
Pencilled Blue	Cape York to Vic
Six Line-blue	Cape York to central NSW
White Line-blue	Cape York to northern NSW
Tailed Green-banded Blue	Cape York to Mackay
Hairy Line-blue	Cape York to southern NSW
Large Green-banded Blue	Cape York to Townsville
Small Green-banded Blue	Cape York to southern NSW
Pea Blue	Mainland Australia
Zebra Blue	Cape York to southern NSW
Common Grass Blue	Australia-wide
Tiny Grass Blue	Darwin to central NSW

Best Host Plants for the Garden	Lays in
Capparis (caper trees)	Sun, shade
Capparis (caper trees)	Sun, shade
Capparis (caper trees)	Sun, shade
Capparis (caper trees)	Sun, shade
Drypetes deplanchei	Sun, shade
Drypetes acuminata	Shade
Mistletoe – many species and all are useful for some butterflies	Shade, sun
Wilkiea macrophylla	Shade
Mucuna gigantea	Shade, sun
Millettia pinnata (Pongamia)	Sun
Palms	Sun, shade
Ficus opposita (sandpaper fig)	Sun, shade
Flowers and foliage of many orchids	Shade, sun
Flowers of *Alphitonia excelsa*	Sun
Seed of *Harpullia pendula, Harpullia ramiflora*	Sun, shade
Salacia disepala	Shade, sun
Brachychiton acerifolius (flame tree)	Sun, shade
Brachychiton acerifolius, Castanospermum australe (black bean)	Sun, shade
Aryrtera divaricata	Sun, shade
Myrsine variabilis	Shade, sun
Entada (matchbox bean)	Sun, shade
Cupaniopsis anacardioides	Sun, shade
Connarus conchocarpus	Shade
Alphitonia excelsa	Sun, shade
Flowering herbs, shrubs, trees and vines in the pea family: eggs are laid on the flower buds	Sun, shade
Plumbago (including cultivated varieties)	Sun
Small flowering plants in pea family, including clover	Sun, shade
Hemigraphis (Australia's smallest butterfly)	Sun, shade

The beautiful Blue Argus butterfly is found in the top end of Northern Territory and Western Australia as well as eastern Queensland. It is an open forest species and usually rests on the ground with wings open.

The Common Jezabel is one of the mistletoe feeding butterflies. It is mostly found in rainforest though is a common garden butterfly in eastern Australia, up to 100km inland, reaching Victoria at times. The larvae use a wide range of mistletoes.

The heavily camouflaged Evening Brown is the only butterfly that flies at night, though usually mostly at dusk. It occurs in the top end of Northern Territory and eastern Australia down to about central New South Wales.

The Blue-banded Eggfly occurs in the top end of Northern Territory and eastern Queensland. It is a rainforest butterfly and the larvae feed on Pseuderanthemum variabile. The males are territorial and usually rest upside down with wings outspread.

The elusive Four-bar Swordtail is rarely seen by butterfly enthusiasts because the adults have a very short life and are often on the wing for only a few weeks each year. This delicate little butterfly is found in the top end of Northern Territory and eastern Australia south to about central New South Wales.

INDEX

FURTHER READING

Anstis, M. 2013. *Tadpoles and Frogs of Australia*. New Holland Publishers, Sydney.

Framenau, V.W., Baehr, B.C., and Zborowski, P. 2014. *A Guide to the Spiders of Australia*. New Holland Publishers, Sydney.

Slater, P., Slater, P., and Slater, R. 2009. *The Slater Field Guide to Australian Birds*. Second Edition. New Holland Publishers, Sydney.

Van Dyck, S., Gynther, I., and Baker, A. 2013. *Field Companion to Mammals of Australia*. New Holland Publishers, Sydney.

Wilson, S. and Swan, G. 2010. *A Complete Guide to Reptiles of Australia*. Third Edition. New Holland Publishers, Sydney.

Zborowski, P. and Storey, R. 2010. *A Field Guide to Insects of Australia*. Third Edition. New Holland Publishers, Sydney.